Schools and Families:
Issues and Actions

Schools and Families: Issues and Actions

Dorothy Rich

nea **PROFESSIONAL LIBRARY**
National Education Association
Washington, D.C.

Copyright © 1987
National Education Association of the United States
The Home and School Institute

Note

The opinions expressed in this publication should not be construed as representing the policy or position of the National Education Association. Materials published as part of the Parent Involvement Series are intended to be discussion documents for teachers who are concerned with specialized interests of the profession.

Library of Congress Cataloging-in-Publication Data

Rich, Dorothy
  Schools and families.

  Bibliography: p.
  1. Home and school—United States.   2. Parent-teacher relationships—United States.   3. School children—United States—Family relationships.   I. National Education Association of the United States.   II. Title.
  LC225.3.R535   1987   371.1'03   87–18601

CONTENTS

Preface 7

Chapter 1. The Significance of Family Involvement 9
    Increased Student Achievement.. 9
    Home Learning Activities 10
    Improved Student Behavior... 11
    Family Acceptance... 12
    Benefits to Parents... 13
    Teacher Acceptance 14
    Benefits to Teachers 14
    Benefits to the Community 15
    Basic Involvement Models.. 16
    Translating Research into Action.................................... 17

Chapter 2. What People Want from Schools 18
    Public Perspectives 19
    Parents Today: The Widening Gap..................................... 20
        Parent Concerns.. 21
    Schools and and the Needs of Families 22
    Student Perspectives 23
    Teacher Perspectives 23
        Student Behavior 23
        Importance of the Home 24
        Home-School Interaction.. 24
    Teachers and Parents: Similar People 24

Chapter 3. Recommendations for Action:
              Programs and Policies 26
    Family 26
    Teachers/Schools 29
    Community.. 32
    Overall Considerations.. 33

Chapter 4. How Family Demographics Can Affect Schools............. 36
   Family Changes and Their Implications
   for Educational Policy.. 36
      Parents and Children 36
   School Children: Current Numbers
   and Future Predictions... 40

Chapter 5. Home Learning Activities....................................... 44
   Sample Activities 45
      Developing Discipline 46
      Thinking and Reasoning 47
      Alcohol and Tobacco.. 48

Appendixes 51
   A. Families as Educators 53
   B. References and Reports on Family Involvement.................... 70
   C. Issues and Emphases of the Parent Involvement Movement 91
   D. Opinion 109
   E. Recommendations for Policymakers............................... 113
   F. Educational Partnerships 118

Bibliography... 122

Selected Resources for Further Study 126

Additional Readings 127

PREFACE

This guide defines policies and programs that help families contribute to and support educational excellence. It presents ways to mobilize schools and families to work together in educational partnerships. The strategies it offers are designed for educational leaders, policymakers, staff, and constituents—for all who are concerned with the role of policy in enhancing the nation's education programs.

The content selected for this guide is based on four major goals for policy and program action to help—

1. Increase awareness of what can be done to recognize and build upon the strengths of the family in reinforcing and expanding upon the work of the school.
2. Unite the efforts of families and teachers in support of children's education.
3. Move from fragmentary "one-shot" efforts to a more systematic, long-range approach by schools to support the educational role of the family.
4. Foster a sense of community in support of schooling and the achievement of all children.

This publication does not deal with such problems as child abuse and neglect, student pregnancy, drug and alcohol abuse, or eating disorders. For information on these topics, see the NEA Combat Series, listed in the Additional Readings section (*How Schools Can Help Combat Child Abuse and Neglect, How Schools Can Help Combat Student Pregnancy, How Schools Can Help Combat Student Drug and Alcohol Abuse*, and *How Schools Can Help Combat Student Eating Disorders*), and/or contact the NEA Professional Library (1201 16th Street, NW, Washington, DC 20036).

—Dorothy Rich

The Author

Dorothy Rich is the founder and president of the Home and School Institute. A nonprofit educational organization based in Washington, D.C., HSI works to link the resources of the school, the home, and the community for student academic achievement and school success. Since 1964 HSI has developed an innovative approach to community involvement in education by providing a structured tutoring role for the family that complements but does not duplicate the work of the school. HSI developed the Teacher-Parent Partnership Project for NEA, as well as the NEA Professional Library multimedia training program *Schools and Parents United: A Practical Approach to Student Success.*

The Advisory Panel

Kathleen W. Corrao, teacher, Brookfield Elementary School, Vermont

F. C. Ellenburg, Professor of Professional Laboratory Experiences, School of Education, Georgia Southern College, Statesboro

Frances Lovell, Instructor of Reading and English, New River Community College, Dublin, Virginia

Stanley M. Lucas, Mathematics teacher (retired), Gainesville High School, Florida

Myrna H. Slick, Librarian, Vocational/Technical School, Johnstown, Pennsylvania

John W. Taylor, Associate Professor of English Linguistics, South Dakota State University, Brookings

Sueann J. West, Guidance Counselor, Bel Air Middle School, Maryland

Chapter 1
THE SIGNIFICANCE OF FAMILY INVOLVEMENT

The relationship between family and school is comparable to that of the right and left hemispheres of the brain. Both are necessary to each other—complementary, nonduplicative, unique, and vital. This is the home-school partnership, ideally envisioned. This chapter provides the information base toward the fulfillment of this ideal. It summarizes the findings of a number of studies of the last two decades concerning the strategic educational function of the family, including the specific roles the family can play, as well as the benefits to students, parents, teachers, and community resulting from the home-school partnership. (For additional information, see Appendix B, References and Reports on Parent Involvement.)

INCREASED STUDENT ACHIEVEMENT

Equality of Educational Opportunity, the Coleman report for the U.S. Office of Education (6),* found the correlation between achievement and family background stronger than the correlation between achievement and "school quality." The report was widely interpreted to mean that "schools don't count; it's the family that counts." Although this interpretation is an oversimplification, the report did help to emphasize that what children bring to school—background and environment—is critically important in the learning process.

A later study, *Parent Involvement in Compensatory Edu-*

---

*Numbers in parentheses appearing in the text refer to the Bibliography beginning on page 122.

cation Programs (46), assessed the major roles of parent involvement that developed in the 1960s. It found in general that the evidence supported participation of "parents-as tutors" of their children. In another study, *Parents as Teachers of Young Children* (14), the authors found that "As a group, the program involving parents as teachers consistently produced significant immediate gains in children's IQ scores, and seemed to alter in a positive direction the teaching behavior of parents."

Several other researchers reported similar results. Urie Bronfenbrenner, reviewing a variety of intervention programs (3), concluded that the active involvement of the family is critical to children's school success. It reinforces and helps sustain the effects of school programs. Theodore Wagenaar, in his study of a large Midwestern school system (48), determined that there was a connection between schoolwide achievement and the level of community involvement and support. Ira Gordon, researching the Follow Through Program (15), concluded that all forms of parent involvement help, but that the more comprehensive the involvement—that is, the more roles parents can play in a school—and the longer this involvement lasts, the more effective it will be. And preliminary results of Joyce Epstein's Maryland study (11) indicate that students whose teachers were leaders in parent involvement made greater gains in reading achievement than did other students. Similar gains in mathematics achievement were not found. Epstein's explanation—the most popular parent involvement practices are reading activities (11).

HOME LEARNING ACTIVITIES

Home learning activities have been a core component in all Home and School Institute (HSI) programs for families for two decades. These activities provide a structured tutoring role for the family that deliberately does not duplicate the work of the school. They are not traditional schoolwork. They teach the basic motivation, skills, and attitudes children need to do well in school, such as improving self-discipline and study habits, and building self-esteem. Readers who wish to know where such parent involvement home learning programs are in place should contact the Home and School Institute (Special Projects Office, 1201 16th Street, NW, Washington, DC 20036). The Institute will refer you to contact persons in selected school systems across the nation.

Test score gains that have emerged from short-term projects provide strong indicators of what may be found in longitudinal studies. For example, after using eight home learning activities, first grade children scored significantly higher on standardized reading tests than did the control group (42). In Project HELP, after a program of learning activities sent home weekly, children, who initially had the lowest scores of all groups studied, made reading gains equal to those of other groups who started at higher levels (4).

And a third study, using the HSI model in special education in the inner city, showed a highly significant increase in children's reasoning skills as well as an increase of over three grade levels in visual-aural skills (20). The majority of special education youngsters who participated in this project are now mainstreamed into regular classrooms.

Compared with other programs in education, however, there have been very few in parent involvement. More data are needed to document even more clearly what works consistently for which students, for what skills, at what grades.

IMPROVED STUDENT BEHAVIOR

Epstein's research suggests that important consequences for student achievement, attitudes, and behavior occur when teachers make parent involvement part of their regular teaching practices. Students reported that they have more positive attitudes toward school and more regular homework habits, that the teacher knows the family, and that they are assigned more homework on weekends (11).

In a recent survey by Collins and others of home-school partnership programs in the upper elementary and secondary schools in 24 large American cities, 28 programs improved the school performance and social development of children. The survey reported reduced absenteeism, higher achievement scores, improved student behavior, and restored confidence and participation among parents (7).

FAMILY ACCEPTANCE

Although tutorial behaviors and roles have been most commonly associated with educated parents and middle-class lifestyles, R. J. Dave found that research and the experience of many programs working with disadvantaged and minority families confirm that educational attainment need not be a barrier to parents in tutoring their children (8).

Other research field experience indicates that family concern for education can be readily translated into practical support for children and for schools. HSI projects have served low socioeconomic families in the District of Columbia, Michigan, Maryland, California, South Carolina, and Virginia, as well as special education and multilingual populations. A brief summary of family participation in three of these programs follows.

- *Project AHEAD* (Accelerating Home Education and Development), developed for the Southern Christian Leadership Conference West, serves 5,000 children, primarily Black and Hispanic, in grades K–3 with a parent-to-parent approach. Results show significant increases in scores in second and third grades on the California Tests of Basic Skills (CTBS). Ninety-seven percent of the parents indicated they wanted to stay in the program, which has been adopted by the Los Angeles Unified School District (41).

- *Families Learning Together*, for simultaneous adult and child learning, served families with children in grades K–6. The participation rate was 77 percent of the total school population. Ninety-eight percent of the parents said they personally learned useful skills and knowledge from the program; 98.5 percent said they felt more confident in working with their own child at home (21).
- In the *Multilingual School Success Project,* a series of family learning activities was developed and translated into Spanish, Vietnamese, Khmer, and Lao for families of children in grades 4–6. The data show a family participation rate of nearly 90 percent across a full semester of activities (47).

BENEFITS TO PARENTS

Epstein analyzed survey responses to determine how teacher practices involving parents affected parents. According to her results, parents whose children's teachers were leaders in parent involvement were more likely than other parents to report the following: they recognized that the teacher worked hard to interest parents in the instructional program; they received most of their ideas for home involvement from the teachers; they felt they should help their children at home; they understood more during the current year than during the previous one about what their child was being taught in school (12).

Parents themselves have spoken of the impact of the activity programs on their children and on how changes in their children made changes in their own lives:

> "The whole family has enjoyed these activities. I think they have helped me in a way more than they have helped my child in that I am developing more patience."
>
> "My child is willing to assume more responsibility and that helps me." (21)

TEACHER ACCEPTANCE

Generally, teachers and administrators have not been enthusiastic about parent participation in curriculum development, instruction, or school governance. Williams reported that they supported other forms of parent involvement, such as assisting with homework or tutoring children, but they felt that teachers should give parents ideas about how to work together on such activities. However, parents expressed interest in taking a more active role than professionals were ready to provide (50).

In 1984, the home activity model was designed for use by the National Education Association in the Teacher-Parent Partnership Project. Third grade teachers in 11 different local associations selected for the program volunteered to send weekly activities home to families. All first-year sites were interested in continuing, and 12 new sites in 1985 opted to participate in the project (33).

BENEFITS TO TEACHERS

An effective parent involvement program does what its name says—it involves parents and does not overburden teachers. As the first-year evaluation report on the multilingual home activity project noted:

> For the teachers, the major benefits have been increased parental involvement with their child's school experiences. The teachers report that more parents came to school conferences than would come to school functions and programs, and more parents would contact the school regarding their child's absence from school or aspects of their child's school work. This finding was very clear for the teachers. (47)

And as one teacher said to the evaluator:

> This project has helped pull parents into the school. The parents of my kids have been unusually involved this year, not just in coming to school for programs and parent conferences

but they're calling more and sending more notes. I also sense they are looking at the homework more than last year. (47)

Parent involvement programs also help teachers receive higher ratings from parents. In Maryland, Epstein found that—

> Parents who participated in involvement programs were more positive about the teacher's interpersonal skills, and rated the teacher higher in overall teaching ability... In other words, teachers who work at parent involvement are considered better teachers than those who remain more isolated from the families of the children they teach. (12)

BENEFITS TO THE COMMUNITY

Finding ways for schools to establish family support for education is a strategic use of scarce public resources. A minor input of school staff time and materials makes major output of parent support possible. Getting help from families means building a stronger educational and political base.

The following findings are significant in that they point to potential trends:

- *Cost*—A study of the cost effectiveness of the Benton Harbor, Michigan, Project HELP indicated that children in this program, at a cost of $4.31 per student, demonstrated gains equal to or exceeding those of students in Title I "Pull-Out Instruction," which cost $565 per student (4).
- *Morale*—According to Urie Bronfenbrenner, one of the designers of the Head Start program:

> One of the most important things we see happening is that not only do parents become more effective as parents, but they become more effective as people. It's a matter of higher self-esteem. Once they saw they could do something about their child's education, they saw they could also do something about housing, their community, and their jobs. (38)

BASIC INVOLVEMENT MODELS

A new parent involvement approach by government—in keeping with the needs of today's schools and families—is necessary. The basic parent involvement models to date are as follows:

- *Parents as Volunteers*—Volunteerism offers extra person power in the classroom. Managed effectively, it can give teachers more teaching time. At its best, this method provides active roles for parents, but volunteers help students in general, not necessarily their own children.
- *Parents as Receivers of Information about the School*—Parent-school communication usually consists of report cards, conferences, and newsletters to keep parents informed. Most of this communication is initiated by the school; parents play relatively passive roles.
- *Parents Working at the School*—Few working parents today can participate in parent advisory committees. A major U.S. Department of Education study of parent involvement in ESEA Title I, ESEA Title VII Bilingual Program, Follow Through, and the Emergency School Aid Act found that the advisory council as a model for involvement was not effective (5).
- *Parents Working with Their Own Children at Home*—Parent education and training involve teaching parents how to improve their family life and/or how to work with their children. Of all the models identified, this one offers the most substantive research to date and is the most appropriate for widespread involvement of families.

TRANSLATING RESEARCH INTO ACTION

Epstein's studies (11, 12) not only support parent involvement as having positive impact upon achievement and school performance, but also provide insight into the feasibility of implementing parent involvement programs in the schools. According to Epstein:

> Almost all parents believe parent involvement is important, but most parents cannot or do not become involved at school. Over 40 percent of the mothers in this sample worked full time and 18 percent worked part time. In contrast, almost all parents were involved at least once in a while in learning activities at home. Over 85 percent reported that they spend 15 minutes or more helping their child at home when asked to do so by the teacher, and that they could spend more time if shown how to help. (12)

And testifying before a Congressional committee, Epstein stated: "If teachers had to choose only one policy to stress, these results suggest that the most payoff for the most parents and students will come from teachers involving parents in helping their children in learning activities at home." (11).

The research and HSI experience suggest that priority attention should be given to developing the mode of participation that directly involves parents in the education of their own child. This is often referred to as the "parent-as-tutor" approach. The reasons for this position are twofold. First, this is the approach that the research cited at the beginning of this chapter indicates is most directly linked to improved academic achievement. Second, this approach offers greater access and opportunity for parent involvement and for sustained participation. Programs that require attendance at meetings or at school activities during the day will necessarily have limited participation. The need to reach out to single parents and to families in which both parents work is a special concern. Furthermore, the parent-as-tutor approach appeals to the most basic parental motivation for involvement—the desire to help one's child do better. (See Appendix A for a detailed discussion of families as educators of their own children.)

Chapter 2
WHAT PEOPLE WANT FROM SCHOOLS

The days when education was a process outside and separate from the family are over. At least four significant, sometimes contradictory, changes are occurring:

1. Not long ago, it was thought that schools were the sources of most information. People attended school to start learning. This is no longer true. Today, it is known that children learn both before and after attending school.
2. The age of experts is increasingly giving way to ideas of self-help. Many people outside school, including parents, have as much formal education as teachers. This is a major change.
3. Information is now available to everyone simultaneously. Teachers learn about current events and new scientific discoveries at the same time everyone learns about them.
4. Parents are again looking to the schools to deal with more than academic problems. Working parents are asking schools to address child care needs. Parents of teenagers look to schools for advice about drug and sex issues. Single parents look to schools as one of their only ongoing institutional ties (10).

Among the implications of these changes for the home-school partnership—parents and teachers want and need different kinds of support from each other.

This chapter provides an overview, gleaned from recent polls, of what parents and teachers are saying about their needs. These issues of public concern are useful indicators to policymakers of what people are thinking. It is important to note, however, that although no consensus of opinion exists, certain trends are emerging. (See Appendix C for a discussion of some of the issues and emphases of the parent involvement movement and school renewal.)

PUBLIC PERSPECTIVES

A review of the Phi Delta Kappa *Gallup Polls of Attitudes Toward Education 1969–1984* indicates that while the public is making demands on the schools, it has not definitely withdrawn support from schools or teachers (39). In 1985, 43 percent of those interviewed gave their schools a grade of A or B (40). The impression gained from the responses over the years is that neither the general public nor parents want to run the schools personally, but there is clear indication that both groups want some measure of involvement. A number of survey questions (39) affected the following family/school issues:

- *Child Care*—Seventy-six percent of parents felt schools should provide activities at school and after school, especially for children from single- and working-parent families, rather than have these children return to empty homes.
- *Preschool and Kindergarten Programs*—Support for early education programs reached 83 percent if paid for by the parents of the children participating in them.
- *Counseling Help for Single-Parent Families*—Eighty-six percent of the respondents thought it was a good idea to have schools open in the evenings to counsel single parents whose children may be having trouble in school.

The message that comes across clearly through all the questions is that parents feel responsible for their children— even to the extent of feeling responsible for the decline in standardized test scores. This sense of strong involvement is probably one of the most hopeful signs for the future.

PARENTS TODAY: THE WIDENING GAP

The original baby boom children are now parents. Their generation is made up of economically disparate parent groups. They are different from their own parents, says social scientist Arthur Wise, in that they know more about schools, they have more money, they are generally more sophisticated, and the mothers are continuing to work (24).

These are the parents who have searched for and found preschool care for their children. They know the questions to ask. They are willing to pay for the services they need. They are also worried about their children and are not sure they are doing the right thing. In addition, they can be difficult for school personnel who are not accustomed to working with parents. If necessary, if they can afford it, these parents may turn to private schools to get what they want.

But this is also the generation of parents who have a growing number of children in poverty. Almost half of all Black children live below the government poverty level, as do 40 percent of Hispanic children. School enrollment in 23 of the 25 largest cities in America is now composed of 70 percent minority students. By the end of the decade, large city schools will serve minority youngsters almost exclusively. More than a third will be non-English-speaking students requiring special programs (9).

Consequently, the challenge for schools will be to meet the differing needs of children from rich and poor families, without promoting a new segregation based on students' background and experience. One solution is for schools to reach out and work with parents and to provide for the individualization needed by children through programs involving their families at home. In this way, schools can build on the basic caring that all families, rich or poor, have for their children.

Parent Concerns

There will probably always be some parents who wish the school would do it all, operating 24 hours a day. But the wish list of many parents and teachers who have participated in Home and School Institute conferences on *Single-Parent Families and the Schools* and *Working Parents and Achieving Children* includes changes that are reasonable (19). They focus on the use of the school as a community institution, serving the needs of the community in new and vital ways.

These parents and teachers expressed greater concern about the overall need of the family to function effectively than about the academic function of the school. They discussed education in terms of child care as well as of traditional school roles, viewing these as complementary and inseparable elements. Among their priorities for change were—

- In-service training for teachers and administrators in dealing with today's families, including improved communication between home and school.
- An increased awareness by teachers of the constraints of working single parents, including scheduling of evening meetings and conferences and the need for more positive attitudes about families undergoing separation, divorce, and remarriage.
- An increase in the number of counselors in the schools, especially at the elementary level to deal with changes in today's families.
- Open enrollment policies in which children could attend schools near parents' work.
- The need for quality child care. Conferees called for more preschool, before-school, and after-school care, as well as some type of supervision for older children. The changes included after-school care in which children did not have to leave the school building, care for latchkey children by matching them with nearby senior citizens who are at home, child care courses for parents, and

survival skill courses for students.
- The use of schools as facilitators for support systems for parents. Among the suggestions was the establishment of peer support groups for single parents and working mothers. Schools were asked to mesh services and supports for families with other organizations and to become "a central focus for needed services." (19)

SCHOOLS AND THE NEEDS OF FAMILIES

While most child care attention has focused on the preschool years, Professor Edward Zigler in Congressional testimony has stated that—

> We should not lose sight of the fact that about two-thirds of the need for day care is for school age children (6–11) whose parents both work . . . For this age group, I believe there is a relatively inexpensive solution to the problem. The solution involves parent-school partnerships in which the school buildings, which are already housing these children for most of the day, are used to house them for a few more hours. (52)

Frustrating to families today is the fact that schools still tend to act as if mothers were waiting at home with milk and cookies for children to return, regardless of the time schools open or shut their doors. One example of the lack of planning for the needs of today's families is the schools' reactions to the vagaries of the weather. While safety is an issue when snow and ice cover the ground, schools also tend to close during heat waves. When school officials notify radio stations about closings in midmorning after classes have started, it is almost impossible for working parents to be home. While not all schools are air conditioned, it may be feasible to lower the shades for a quiet read-aloud period so that youngsters may stay in the classrooms. In this way, children remain safe and in a learning environment; parents can finish their day on the job without worrying about their children and their employers; and schools show their concern for family needs.

STUDENT PERSPECTIVES

The National Center for Educational Statistics recently surveyed high school students about the involvement of their parents (31). Students who received mostly A's and B's (all grades were self-reported) indicated a substantially higher parent involvement than those who received C's and D's. Answers given by students with higher grades indicated that—

- Parents almost always know the child's whereabouts.
- The child talks with the mother or father almost every day.
- Parents attend PTA meetings at least once in a while.
- The mother keeps close track of how well the child does in school.

This information can be useful for policymakers interested in how to support the continuing role of the home with students in the high school years.

TEACHER PERSPECTIVES

The National Education Association, through its *Nationwide Teacher Opinion Polls*, surveys teachers regularly on a variety of issues (34, 35, 36, 37). Among the questions asked have been some on the relationship between home and school. The responses offer useful insights about what teachers hope for and need.

Student Behavior

Each year teachers are given a long list of conditions that have been connected with student misbehavior in schools. In 1983, one question asked: "To what extent is each factor or condition responsible for whatever misbehavior there is in your school?" Of all the factors listed, including overcrowded classes, unskilled teachers, and lack of support from principals, the two rated highest by teachers were "Irresponsible Parents" and Unsatisfactory Home Conditions" (34).

Another question asked: "To help alleviate student misbehavior problems, do you support or oppose the following . . . ?" First on the list of measures to alleviate the problem was "Keep parents better informed." In 1980, this ranked highest with 97.4 percent of responses (37). In 1982, this same response received the highest ranking of all, 97.7 percent (35).

Importance of the Home

In 1981, teachers were asked: "Recognizing that both homelife and schools are important, which of the two do you think is more important in determining whether or not a child achieves academically?" Teachers ranked homelife at 87.6 percent, school at 12.4 percent (36). The high ranking of the home could be considered a rationale or copout for the difficulty schools encounter with certain children, but it can also be seen as a recognition of the significance of the home as an educational environment—a recognition that can be mobilized into action.

Home-School Interaction

In the 1981 poll teachers were also asked: "Do you think there needs to be more home-school interaction?" "Yes" was ranked at 93.6 percent over the 6.4 percent ranking for "no" (36).

TEACHERS AND PARENTS: SIMILAR PEOPLE

To an extent perhaps not possible in earlier times, teachers and parents are caring more about each other, not just because of the different roles they play in children's lives, but because they are human beings with similar problems. No longer the town spinster, today the teacher, like the parent, is a person who goes dancing, gets married, has children, needs child care, and even gets divorced. Teachers and parents are therefore in a better position to understand each other's needs. As Sharon Lynn Kagan of the Yale Bush Center writes:

> Parent involvement of the 1980s is becoming characterized by a new give and take. In the 1980s schools face no mandate to bring parents into the schools and parents must be highly motivated to enter. In so doing, they are reforming the relationship between themselves, schools, and communities." (22)

To summarize, then, the traditional ways of responding to and involving families must adapt to these changing attitudes and mandates. Fortunately for everyone, parents and teachers can be helped to find involvement strategies that are appropriate and useful today.

Chapter 3
RECOMMENDATIONS FOR ACTION: PROGRAMS AND POLICIES

This chapter provides recommendations in three areas: *Family, School,* and *Community*. In the context of partnership, recommendations in one area have impact on those in other areas. It should also be mentioned that these recommendations are designed to be illustrative and to provide direction. Individual communities and schools will develop their specific plans to carry them out. (See Appendix E for five specific steps policymakers can take to support the educational role of the family. See also Appendix F for a discussion of educational partnerships, including suggestions for school/community participation.)

FAMILY

1. Support and assign educational responsibilities to the family.

Program development should focus on the methods identified by research as most effective. Federal and state legislation should be amended as necessary to provide for family education programs at the local school level. These programs should emphasize the supportive educational role of the family.

> *Example:* Original ESEA Title I programs were designed with the family/community functioning in an advisory capacity at best. While this may have been a relevant and useful model at the time of its design, it is no longer the most appropriate involvement method because of changes in family life and the findings of educational research. A redirection of this policy at

federal and state levels, to take advantage of the family's educative role, is in order.

2. Provide families with the practical information they need to help educate their children.

Polls underscore parents' readiness to learn more about how to help their children.

> *Example:* Families across the nation need similar kinds of information to help their children learn. Materials should be available for them in easy-to-read, easy-to-use leaflets from every school and also from such locations as doctors' offices and supermarkets. The availability of this information may help prevent the development of many problems—for both parents and teachers.

3. Respond to family diversity and differing parental needs.

Policy should identify strategies to respond to the more complex and diverse nature of families and schooling today. Schools for four-year-olds may be good for some, day care centers and home-based care for others. Home schooling, which has captured headlines, remains a choice for only a few; it does not affect the greater number of families.

Face Up to Child Care Needs: Incentives should be devised for schools and community agencies to help working parents with before- and after-school care of their children close to their place of employment. The needs of working mothers and single parents for such child care can no longer be ignored. They impact upon the amount of time parents spend with their children and the level of parental support for their children's schooling. These concerns for child care and good education are integrated: they are not in conflict.

> *Example:* Some communities have established Workplace Schools with child care as part of the program. In Prince George's County, Maryland, for example, where *Workplace Schools* have been incorporated as part of the county's desegregation plan, parents can sign up for the before- and after-school care that these schools provide.

Support Concern for the Child by the Noncustodial Parent: In most cases, the more parents are involved with the child, the better for the child. Rather than discouraging this interest of noncustodial divorced or separated parents, schools will want to encourage it.

> *Example:* School boards can allocate the additional funds needed for clerical work and postage to ensure that all noncustodial parents who want them receive report cards and school notices. Although this is an extra school task, it may well be one of the least expensive ways that schools can build parent involvement.

4. Encourage an active role for fathers.

Policymakers should find ways to encourage fathers to be more directly involved in the care and education of their children.

> *Example:* A media campaign showing fathers working with children can use public service messages on TV during football games and other sports programs. Such messages enhance the image of the father as caregiver to children, not just family provider. Also, seed money grants can encourage schools and other agencies to provide programs for fathers in their role as educators of their children.

5. Encourage family self-help and self-sufficiency.

Policy should reaffirm strength in all families. The overwhelming majority of parents, regardless of socioeconomic and educational background, possess basic abilities to help their children achieve.

> *Example:* HSI has successfully employed a "nondeficit" approach in its programs for linking families with schools. This approach emphasizes family and child strengths rather than compensation for deficits. Individualized Education Plans (IEPs) in special education programs, mandated by Public Law 94–142, should include Home Education Plans (HEPs) that families can use at home to help their children learn.

6. Provide ways for families to help each other.

Policymakers should find ways to support the work of parent-to-parent programs. In fact, the concept of self-help has been identified as a megatrend (30).

Example: Incentives can be provided for schools to establish peer-support groups for teen parents, as well as for single and working parents. Groups such as Parents Without Partners can be encouraged to organize and hold meetings at the school and to focus on school-family concerns.

A parent-to-parent approach has at least three special benefits:

- It provides fast, needed personal help to families under special stress—attention that might not be readily available from usually overburdened social service systems.
- It removes the burden from the school as the focus for all support and help for families. Schools cannot be expected to provide all the educational and social services that families need. Parents helping each other assume responsibilities for self-help and act as resources to one another.
- It helps to restore a sense of community and of friendship from one family to another. This is much missed today when children attend school far from home and parents work many miles away. Parent-to-parent support helps to restore the sense of neighborhood.

TEACHERS/SCHOOLS

1. Support family involvement as an integral and funded part of the schools' services.

Schools should recognize the family as a system—for teaching and learning. It is not enough to work with the child alone.

Example: Increases in teacher salaries can be linked to expectations that they will work with families, that they will facilitate family learning and collaborative decision making with adults.

Designate Home-School Liaison Workers: Professionals or paraprofessionals should be funded to coordinate and integrate the efforts of home and school at local school sites.

> *Example:* Policymakers can designate funds for local schools to hire, at least on a half-time basis, home-school liaison workers to connect the work of schools and families in the education of children. Training should be provided to these new workers or to reassigned personnel doing this work in such areas as teacher support, family learning, and family outreach. Community agencies can nominate persons to become home-school liaisons.

2. Provide teachers with training and information to help them work well with families.

Teachers should receive needed training and materials to help them work more closely and effectively with today's families. Part of this new and enhanced role for teachers is to coordinate what is learned outside the classroom with what is learned inside. This means working with adults as well as with children.

> *Example:* Experience with HSI School and Family-Community Involvement training for educators indicates that teachers have not been prepared for work with families. They need to become familiar with the research about families as educators, and they need to learn the strategies for reaching and teaching adults. Providing this know-how to new teachers should be expected from and included in current teacher training programs. These programs can be designed so that teachers on the job can participate in half-day sessions to gain the necessary skills.

3. Provide for family involvement at all levels of schooling.

Policy should support different kinds of parent involvement programs for the middle school and high school years. The family involvement of the elementary grades is not appropriate for the secondary school years. Studies indicate that teens still view their parents as the most influential people in their lives, but communication between teen and parent is often difficult (1). Programs can be provided to help parents and youngsters communicate, to help parents express care and concern on a more adult-to-adult basis. Such programs have potential for combating the dropout problem caused in part when teens feel that no one cares any more and that their schooling is meaningless.

> *Example:* Programs in the secondary school years, such as the HSI *Job Success Begins at Home* (see Selected Resources for Further Study), address the needs of teens to grow up and of parents to have them grow up—to learn about jobs, mortgages, taxes, and other adult responsibilities.

4. Use school facilities for community needs.

Policy should support the increased use of school facilities to serve a wide range of community needs. Schools can begin to position themselves to be not a supplier of all services, but a focus and facilitator of learning for the community.

> *Example:* Separate staff can be hired to provide before- and after-school care for youngsters, to run summer programs, and to involve seniors as caregivers to latchkey children. The possibilities are unlimited.

Carefully articulated, this new focus will not extend the work of the school. On the contrary, it will extend the impact of the school as an important educational resource for old and young, before and after school hours, all year long.

5. Find ways to coordinate teacher/school schedules to the work schedules of today's families.

Policymakers, especially at the local level, should seek ways to overcome the barriers between home and school caused by conflicting schedules of working parents and teachers.

> *Example:* Teachers and school boards in a number of districts have contracts providing that parent/teacher conferences be held in the evenings and at other times when parents can attend. This is made possible by restructuring teacher time, or using substitutes, and by providing child care.

6. Emphasize early prevention of learning problems.

Policy should focus as much or more on prevention as on remedial programs. Information programs should be developed to increase public awareness about the family, the many roles and services it provides, its basic strengths, and the challenges and problems families today encounter.

> *Example:* The mass media, particularly television, should be used to create a better awareness of the family's impact on learning. Print materials to help families work with their children should be distributed from supermarkets, churches and temples, gas stations—not just from schools.

COMMUNITY

1. Provide meaningful roles for the private sector.

Business should be provided with information and materials to offer support for the family-school relationship. The choices for private employers to help parents are not limited to setting up child care centers.

> *Example:* Policymakers should consider ways to encourage the contributions of business to the work of the schools. In addition to serving as classroom volunteers, employees can be given time to participate in parent-teacher conferences. And employers can distribute parenting information that helps employees reduce stress due to work/home conflicts.

2. Connect community agencies in collaborative efforts to reach families.

Policy should stimulate schools to form collaborative arrangements with other agencies in the community. One way to do this is to offer teachers incentives to work with mental health agencies, community groups, business, the media, etc.

> *Example:* Seed money grants should be provided to teachers to develop local school/community educational networks. Community groups, such as the NAACP, the PTA, and AARP can join with teachers to provide services such as counseling and apprenticeships for potential dropouts.

3. Involve senior citizens and nonparents in educational activities.

Older people should be involved with schools, families, and children. Not only do they have a great deal to offer, but their assistance is much needed. They provide helping hands to teachers in classrooms and to families in special need. Moreover, the seniors themselves benefit from this constructive role in ongoing community life.

> *Example:* The Older Americans Act provides for employment programs for the elderly to work in community service jobs. RSVP provides for volunteer programs. What is missing in many of these programs is the link connecting seniors to students' families. In the HSI Senior Corps programs, a curriculum was developed specifically to link seniors to families. Field test results indicate that this link is good for everyone involved.

OVERALL CONSIDERATIONS

1. Provide for programs that take advantage of the findings of research and experience, including the continuation of programs judged effective.

Policy should encourage using what has already been learned, rather than encouraging the development of new programs in every instance. Schools need to learn from one another. The involvement of the private sector can help schools continue effective programs.

> *Example:* Family involvement programs that help to build students' basic skills and improve self-discipline are of interest to the business community, which has a stake in the availability of a local work force that is literate and employable. Business is increasingly coming to understand education as an investment; schools can build on this view by providing local businesses with information about needed programs in order to encourage their interest and cooperation.

2. Provide support for complementary efforts of schools, families, and community groups.

Start with Children's Earliest Years: Policy should support information for parents about their significant educative role from the time of their child's birth.

> *Example:* Education for successful schooling can begin with in-hospital programs as new parents receive practical tips and information on how they can help their infants develop optimally.

Integrate Education in Family Day Care: Policymakers should support education programs for children in family day care. The majority of early childhood care in this country is being offered in family day care homes: it is recognized that before-school education is vital to the success of children in school (3).

> *Example:* Educational training for family day care providers can be offered in their own living rooms through community cable television and other local access means. To provide incentives, these day care givers can obtain accreditation for successful participation in such programs.

3. Include evaluation so that programs can be judged effective or ineffective.

Programs should include funding for evaluation and research in order to overcome the limitations of current knowledge about family involvement and schools.

> *Examples:* Current data on the impact of working mothers/single parents on children's achievement are limited not only by the brief number of years in which they have been studied but also by the fact that the data are drawn mainly from studies that were not specifically focused on the direct link between family life and children's school achievement.
>
> There is a real need for data that show the relation of family life to the achievement of children in school, and the kinds of impact programs have on families and schools.

4. Encourage sharing of what has been accomplished.

Policy should ensure that information about school accomplishments, particularly those involving families, is widely disseminated through the media and at local civic and community group meetings. The accomplishments of the system and its students are community achievements. They should be presented in that light, so that everyone feels a sense of success.

> *Example:* Academic departments can learn from sports departments about how to publicize programs. In these academic programs parents are the coaches: they can be interviewed, news releases and features can be sent to the media. The goal is to build community support not only for increased funding to support a school budget or a bond issue, but to build morale—a feeling in each member of the community that "I can do it!"

The preceding recommendations represent new choices and responsibilities for families and schools. Parents today are accustomed to some level of control and decision making over their lives and the lives of their children. To be effective, then, policies must provide such choices and opportunities for all families.

Chapter 4
HOW FAMILY DEMOGRAPHICS CAN AFFECT SCHOOLS

FAMILY CHANGES AND THEIR IMPLICATIONS FOR EDUCATIONAL POLICY

This chapter presents 14 questions and answers that have been compiled to assist policymakers and staff in addressing family demographic changes and in formulating policy for school/family needs in the near future. (See also Appendix E.) Supplementary references are provided in Additional Readings.

Parents and Children

Q: How many mothers are employed?
A: About 62 percent of married women with children under 18 years of age were in the labor force in 1985, but many of them worked only part time. Twenty-nine percent of all married mothers work full time year-round. By contrast, 63 percent of all divorced mothers work full time (2).

The new or most prevalent "traditional" family is one with an employed mother who works at least part time outside the home. This is confirmed by the fact that about half of all married women with children under six were in the labor force in 1985 on at least a part-time basis (2).

Q: Do children of working mothers/two-parent households perform less well in school?
A: A review of studies by the National Academy of Sciences has concluded that, in general, the school achievement of

children of working mothers differs little from that of the children of nonworking mothers (23).

- Children's development is influenced by many factors. The mother's employment is only one of these and not necessarily the most important.
- Employment is not a single uniform condition. It is not experienced in the same way by all parents, and it does not affect all children in the same way.
- In the National Academy of Sciences study, the advice given is: "Don't ask if working parents are good or bad for kids because the answer is 'It depends.' It depends on the parents, on the child, on the circumstances, and so forth."

A recent national study of elementary and secondary school students suggests a caution. In two-parent white families, children whose mothers were employed had lower achievement than those with nonemployed mothers, even after allowing for the influence of various other relevant factors. The size of the effect was directly related to the amount of time mothers worked. These findings show that both single-parent families and working mothers in two-parent families can have negative effects on school achievement, but results differ by age, race, and family structure. The results also demonstrate the importance of mediating variables such as income and time use (29).

Q: Does the fact that a mother works limit her involvement in her child's education?

A: Working poses some limitation on the mothers' participation in school activities, but many mothers make significant efforts to maintain close contacts with teachers and schools (27). There is a decline in parent-school activities that do not include the child or allow for contact with the child. Given time conflicts, working parents may be less visible and active in school activities during the day (25).

In light of the available data, it seems unlikely that work status in and of itself accounts for a significant variance in student achievement or level of parent participation in school.

Q: Do working mothers spend less time with their children?

A: Studies of time use suggest that working mothers spend almost as much time caring for their children as do nonworking mothers (18).

The working mother who is "time poor" seems to work harder at maintaining some level of activity involving child and spouse, eliminating personal leisure time instead (28).

Q: Do workplace policies affect the participation of mothers in education-related activities?

A: When leave policies are rigid and job stress is high, mothers in dual earner families have lower involvement in their children's education (13). Flextime is available to only a small percentage of full-time workers.

Q: How many single-parent families are there?

A: One-parent families now account for 26 percent of all families in the nation with children under 18. That total was 13 percent in 1970. About 50 percent of Black children live with one parent (44).

Q: Is the overall intellectual functioning of children harmed in single-parent homes?

A: A review of studies done for the National Institute of Education (NIE) shows that when the socioeconomic status of families is taken into account, the intelligence of children in one- and two-parent households is similar. Aptitude and achievement test scores are lower for those from one-parent homes, but the differences are not large (17). Wilson and Hernstein summarize the impact of the "broken home" as follows: "The safest conclusion is that the central features of family life—a fortunate biological endowment, secure attachments, and consistent discipline—are more important than whether it is a two-parent family, one with a working mother, or one in which corporal punishment is fequently employed" (51).

Q: Do children from single-parent households have more difficulty in school?

A: The same review of studies for NIE shows that children from one-parent homes do tend to receive lower grades, display more disruptive behavior in school, and have poorer attendance (17).

Q: Which single-parent children do better in school?

A: *Sex Differences*: Although the adjustment of both sexes was similar at the time of divorce, girls were much better adjusted than boys one year later. Yet girls were not treated much differently from boys by their teachers (49). Many studies suggest that the impact of marital discord and divorce on emotional and social adjustment is more pervasive and enduring for boys than for girls (17).

Age Differences: Children who are very young when their parents divorce fare better psychologically than their older siblings. Five years after the marriage breakup, younger children in the study appeared to be more depressed than older siblings. But after 10 years, younger children remembered fewer stressful events while older children suffered continued damaging memories (49).

Q: Does being a single parent lessen home-school involvement?

A: Single parents talk with teachers as frequently as do other parents (16). Children of one- and two-parent backgrounds are equally likely to spend time with parents on schoolwork.

Across white, Black and Hispanic families, over 75 percent of all mothers were judged to be moderately or highly involved in the education of their children (13).

For mothers who do not work, there is a difference between white and Black families regarding help in school activities. When they have no husband at home, white mothers help in school less; but among Black mothers, there is little difference with or without a husband at home (28).

SCHOOL CHILDREN: CURRENT NUMBERS AND FUTURE PREDICTIONS

Q: How many children attend school in the United States today? What numbers can be expected in the near future?

A: In the school year 1985–86, there were 39,468,269 children enrolled in U.S. schools (32).

The first year of the elementary school "bulge," which will really emerge in the next few years was 1985. The peak year for elementary school enrollment is expected to be 1989–1990. Geography is a factor, with the Southwest and Southeast experiencing most of this increase in school population (9).

Enrollments in public elementary schools will increase gradually during the late 1980s as the 5- to 17-year-old population rises from 44 million to almost 52.3 million in the year 2000. Demand for public and private preschool services will continue to rise, as will concerns about these services. The number of children under 8 is expected to peak in the next 15 years, and is likely to flatten out at a level higher than at present. Many of these children will need preschool services almost immediately (9).

Q: How many children live in poverty? What are the implications for schooling?

A: According to the government-defined poverty line—

around $10,600 for a family of four—21.3 percent of all children under 18 live in poverty (43). In society as a whole, 14.4 percent of the population live in poverty. Several decades ago, before social security, the elderly were the poorest group. Today, 12.4 percent of the elderly live in poverty (43).

The reasons for the large numbers of children living in poverty today are as follows:

- The real value of welfare has not kept up with inflation.
- There is higher unemployment among young families and minorities.
- Single-parent families are on the increase and they are poorer than dual-income families. The great majority of single-parent households are headed by women. In a number of cases, divorced mothers are forced to go on welfare or move in with parents or other relatives. The poverty rate is 40 percent for single-parent, female-headed families (43).

Q: What child care needs are indicated for the next decade?

A: *Supervision of Children Beyond School Hours*: Estimates indicate that between 5 and 7 million children age 13 and under whose parents are employed full time are without supervision for a significant part of the day (26). Exact figures are unavailable since many parents do not reveal if their children are unsupervised.

The ASCD (Association for Supervision and Curriculum Development) Elementary Curriculum Trend survey reported that only three of 100 schools offer child care before the school day begins. Only six of 100 offer after-school care (10).

Preschool Needs: The percentage of three- and four-year-olds enrolled in early childhood development programs has almost doubled from 21 percent in 1970 to 38 percent in 1983. Increased demand for these programs cannot be attributed solely to more mothers working outside the home. The enrollment rate for three- and four-year-olds with mothers who are not in the labor force is 32 percent. The popularity of such programs, says the High-Scope Educational Research Foundation, may also be due to recent studies that have underscored the favorable long-term effects of such high-quality preschool child care (45).

There is very little public funding for preschool programs. The major funding source in the United States is the federal government. Yet Head Start, the best-known federal program, has space to serve fewer than 25 percent of eligible youngsters (45). State governments are assuming more responsibility for preschool education. State funding, independent of federal funding, is now legislated in 14 states and at least 15 other states are considering new or expanded legislation for early childhood development programs (45).

Q: Is the family still able to care for and nurture children?

A: Surprising to many is the fact that 70.5 percent of the people in the United States live in households headed by married couples (44). Despite a high divorce rate (far higher than that of any other country), the nation also has a high remarriage rate. This means that at any given time, a high percentage of the population is living in two-parent families.

Recent research has placed the family in a more positive light. It has found that in most families, adults genuinely struggle to be good parents; children and adolescents feel good about their parents; parent-child relationships are more affectionate and supportive than rejecting or hostile; parents and children like to be with each other; and families are relatively immune to such major crises as abuse, drug dependency, or violence (1).

In 1983, the Search Institute in Minneapolis completed its national study of 8,000 young adolescents and 10,000 parents. Among its findings were the following:

- Most young adolescents experience high levels of parental affec-

tion and nurture; three-quarters of young adolescents report that there is a lot of love in their family; and 65 percent feel trusted by their parents.
- Although it is true that peers become more influential between the fifth and ninth grades, and parents become less so, in no grade does the influence of peers outweigh the influence of parents.
- Adults care about being good parents. Only a minority of parents use harsh or extreme methods of punishment. The vast majority worry about how well they are parenting and want programs that will help them improve their parenting skills. (1)

Chapter 5
HOME LEARNING ACTIVITIES

The NEA/HSI Teacher-Parent Partnership Project, begun in 1984-85, builds upon and strengthens educational bonds among children, parents, and teachers. It consists of specifically formulated activities that all parents can use with their children. These activities are not designed to help youngsters pass tomorrow morning's test. They are intended to help children feel more successful by doing a real-life activity together with a parent or other adult. For example, a child may learn to answer the telephone with more confidence, make a wiser decision about buying clothing, or talk with parents about what to watch on TV. Reading, writing, and arithmetic are part of all the activities, but they are not workbook exercises. They are real-life experiences. Descriptions of three activities are given later in this chapter.

In the course of a semester, classroom teachers send these activities—one each week—home with students. Together, children and their parents complete them. Parents return feedback sheets that indicate they have completed the activity. This interaction increases communication among all participants.

The NEA/HSI project is thus designed to help children become more academically motivated and self-disciplined, to provide a framework for parents to work with their children, and to build strong community and parental support for teachers and the role of teaching. (See also Appendix D for a discussion of the importance of the school and the community in home learning.) The project chose third grade because this is a pivotal, academic development year, and also because parent involvement is often lower by this time. In addition to parents, grandparents and other adults are encouraged to participate.

During the first project year, 1984–85, 281 third grade teachers in 140 elementary schools in 10 states were involved, with over 6,000 students voluntarily participating. Families at all the sites answered several questions about their involvement in the program. For example, 91 percent said they used the activity in their home; 99 percent said the activity helped them spend enjoyable time with their child; 98 percent felt their child learned something useful from the project; and 99 percent thought the activity would be helpful to other parents.

Thirteen sites in six regions were selected for participation in 1985–86. Feedback from 96 percent of the parents indicated that the project helped them spend enjoyable time with their children, and they thought other parents should participate. In addition, 99 percent of the children enjoyed doing the activities.

SAMPLE ACTIVITIES

The following pages contain two home learning activities from the NEA/HSI Teacher-Parent Partnership Project ("Developing Discipline" and "Thinking and Reasoning") and one three-part activity from the HSI Senior Corps Program ("Alcohol and Tobacco").

Developing Discipline

"What Show Should We Watch Tonight?"
Making TV Work for Your Family

Why Do It?

There is great concern that most children spend too much time watching television, cutting into time that needs to be spent on homework or sports. This activity encourages thoughtful TV viewing. It helps children to make choices and to practice self-discipline.

Materials Needed

TV guide, pencil, paper, TV set

How to Do It

1. Decide, as a family, to go on a TV "diet" for one week. Together, agree on the amount of time you will spend watching each day. (This might be one or two hours a day. Try not to watch more.)
2. Together, using a weekly TV guide, select the shows you will watch. Make a list of your child's and your choices.
3. Post this list where everyone can see it.
4. Have some family games, puzzles, or other activities ready for non-TV hours. Read a book together or play a game. Don't be tempted to turn on the TV. Try to stick to the plan.
5. Give yourself a reward—a picnic or a special family outing—for sticking to the plan.

More Ideas

Help your child become a TV critic. "I like this show because . . ." or, "I don't like this show because . . ." Keep a world map and other reference books close at hand. Look up countries and places mentioned on news programs.

Helpful Hint

Try to watch TV together as a family. Express your opinions about whether or not you like what you have seen. Sitting together and sharing TV watching is a way to express closeness. Talking about what you see as a family is a way to help children make value judgments.

Thinking and Reasoning

"Yes I Can, No You Can't." Holding a Family Debate

Why Do It

Children often disagree with their parents about rules, seeing only their own point of view. This activity makes it easier for children to consider both sides of an issue, and it can help with everyday family arguments.

How to Do It

1. You and your child choose one rule that causes family arguments—for example, the time the child should go to bed.
2. Ask your child's opinion of the rule. That opinion might be, "Kids should go to bed whenever they want."
3. Ask your child to give at least two reasons for this opinion. For example, "It's more fun." "I miss the best TV shows when I go to bed early." Listen carefully to the child's point of view.
4. Now ask your child to give two arguments against this point of view. One might be, "Parents know how much rest children need." This is called giving pro and con arguments. It is an excellent way to help children learn to consider alternatives before making a decision.
5. While your child is working on these pro and con arguments, you do the same. Explain your points of view to each other. What are the differences? What are the similarities?

More Ideas

Play "What Would You Do If You Were the Parent?" Let the child argue an issue from the viewpoint of the parent; you argue from that of the child.

Hold a family debate. Choose a problem to solve. Divide into teams, one team for the issue, the other against. Allow each team the same amount of time to express its view. Allow time for closing arguments.

Helpful Hint

Talk over your differing points of view. Did you have good points? Do you need to change household rules? Children have been known to be very reasonable when they become involved in helping to make family rules.

Alcohol and Tobacco

False Friends
Keeping Away from Alcohol and Tobacco

Part 1. Teaching tips for the senior aide and suggested ways for the aide also to benefit from doing the activity.

Tips for Aides

Here are tips and ideas that will make it easier for you to do the Aide-Student activity.

- Talk about the bad effects of the continued use of tobacco. Example: Serious lung and heart problems.
- Discuss the bad effects of drinking too much alcohol. Examples: Decrease in judgment and self-control, reduced efficiency at work and at school, danger of accident when driving.
- Talk about early uses for alcohol and tobacco. Examples: Smoking the peace pipe, drinking wine as part of religious rituals.
- Ask what the student thinks about smoking and drinking. Try to listen to the student's point of view without judging. Don't hesitate to express your opinion, but let the youngster know that you are an understanding and interested friend.

Aide: This Benefits You Too!

When you were younger, little was known about the dangers of alcohol and tobacco. You might have started smoking without knowing what the problems were and how difficult it would be to stop. Learn the latest facts about the dangers of drinking and smoking.

Part 2. Directions for a specific activity that the senior aide and the student can do together in the classroom or senior center.

Here are easy-to-do steps for teaching this activity in an informal way.

Gather These Materials

Pen or pencil, paper

Do Together/Take Turns

- Together, think of as many reasons as you can why people drink and smoke. Examples: Curiosity, peer pressure, advertising, boredom.
- Talk about good ways to avoid tobacco and alcohol. Examples: Be well informed about drawbacks; find other ways, such as sports, to relieve tension.
- Tell each other stories about people you know or have heard about who have run into problems because of drinking.

Discussion Sparkers: Ask Students

- In your opinion, should the rights of nonsmokers be considered? Should smoking and nonsmoking sections be set aside in all public places?
- What do you do when you realize that some of your friends are drinking or smoking too much? Do you try to tell them about the dangers?

Part 3. The take-home learning activity for the student to do with parents. Using the same topic, it extends the learning of the classroom activity in a new way.

This home learning activity reinforces what is learned in school. It does this in special ways that do not duplicate schoolwork.

Why Do It

This activity teaches students the potential dangers of drinking and smoking.

Materials Needed

Newspaper, magazine, pen or pencil, paper

Do Together/Take Turns

- Together, try to find an article in the newspaper that tells about an accident or a fire resulting from drinking and smoking (or remember an article you read in the paper earlier).
- Tell what you would have done to avoid this accident.
- Find an ad in a magazine that shows glamorous people drinking or smoking. Do you believe that all the claims an ad makes are true? Talk about the points you don't agree with.

Another Idea

Take a private poll among friends and relatives. Make a list of those who smoke and those who drink socially. Are there more drinkers and smokers than nondrinkers and nonsmokers? Did you find anything surprising in your poll?

APPENDIXES

A. Families as Educators... 53
   "Families as Educators of Their Own Children"
   by Dorothy Rich, James Van Dien, and Beverly Mattox 53

B. References and Reports on Parent Involvement 70
   "Studies of Families as Educators: 1979–86"................. 70
   "Synthesis of Recent Research on Parent Participation
   in Children's Education" by Oliver C. Moles 81

C. Issues and Emphases of the Parent Involvement Movement 91
   "A Child Resource Policy: Moving Beyond Dependence
   on School and Family" by Shirley Brice Heath
   and Milbrey Wallin McLaughlin 91
   "Let's Not Throw Out the Baby with the Bath Water"
   by Dorothy Rich 102
   "A Matter of Interpretation" by Shirley Brice Heath
   and Milbrey Wallin McLaughlin 107

D. Opinion 109
   "The Community Gap in Education Reform"
   by Dorothy Rich 109

E. Recommendations for Policymakers 113
   "Parent Involvement in Education: What Can Policymakers Do?" by Dorothy Rich and James Van Dien 113

F. Educational Partnerships 118
   "Education Requires Partnerships Among Staff,
   Students, and Community" by William J. Simpson
   and Sandra Simpson 118

APPENDIX A. FAMILIES AS EDUCATORS

Note: The following article was written almost a decade ago, in 1979. It reports on studies of the 1970s. Before including it in this appendix, I reread it to find out if it was out of date. What is depressing and discouraging is that what was written in 1979 continues to be true today. Other than the fact that Title I is now called Chapter I and that advisory councils are no longer mandated, the article reads as though it could have been written at the present time. The value of including it in these readings is that it shows how little progress has been made, despite the recognition, the knowledge, and the rhetoric about the importance of parent involvement over the last 10 years. It points out the urgency of taking needed action now. What I hope is that well before another decade is completed, this article will really be out of date.

—Dorothy Rich

FAMILIES AS EDUCATORS OF THEIR OWN CHILDREN*

by Dorothy Rich, James Van Dien, Beverly Mattox

"One parent is worth a thousand teachers."

This ancient Chinese proverb illustrates what many professional educators have always known intuitively and what recent research confirms: the family critically influences the learning of the child.

Schooling rests upon an assumption so fundamental that it is taken for granted. The assumption is that the environment of the home and community is conducive to and supportive of academic achievement. What schooling is able to accomplish depends, more perhaps than has been recognized or admitted, upon the cooperation and support of the home.

In 1978, the Home and School Institute (HSI) conducted a survey of school and family/community practices for the Maryland State Department of Education. Also surveyed were the policy-

---

*Copyright © 1979 by the Home and School Institute. From *Partners: Parents and Schools*, edited by Ronald S. Brandt (Association for Supervision and Curriculum Development, 1979).

making and administrative structures which support the outreach efforts of schools to family and community at the local educational agency (LEA) level. We believe this was a unique effort to look at the extent and variety of programs and practices available within a state.

Some of the key findings from this survey are summarized here,[1] and are useful in providing a picture of how school systems have approached the challenge of family involvement in education. The survey found many programs and a number of "promising practices." Almost all the elements of a comprehensive plan for school and family involvement could be identified as existing somewhere in the state, but not together anywhere.

The following less favorable findings give cause for concern:

1. Very limited support for parents to be directly involved in the education of their children.

2. A general lack of clear policy guidelines and coordinated planning. Responsibilities are often divided among a number of offices. Usually parent involvement is treated as an "extra."

3. Understaffing and underbudgeting for family involvement components. If staff time and budget allotments are good measures of an institution's priorities, family involvement cannot be viewed as a commitment of high order.

4. Proliferation of programs and practices on an ad hoc basis in response to specific needs and problems, with a resulting imbalance in the opportunities available. For example, one school may have a plethora of programs, while another a few miles away may have very little to offer.

5. Preponderant influence of federal programs and guidelines. Title I and Title IV-C programs are heavily represented among those identified as strong and successful. While federal support has permitted the opportunity for the expansion of activities and experimentation, it raises the question as to what extent practices would be institutionalized and supported at the local level if federal supports were withdrawn. A corollary to this is the predominance of advisory councils, mandated under federal guidelines, as a favored mode of participation.

6. Lack of solid evaluation of family involvement programs and practices. This, of course, is directly related to the limited

staffing and budget support available. Much of the data available is the reporting of gross numbers participating with little attention given to quality of program, elements of success, or impact.

7. Pivotal influence of the principal at the building level. What happens with regard to parent involvement in a particular school is in large part determined by the philosophy and the priorities of the principal.

8. Lack of programs at the secondary level. Generally speaking the opportunities for involvement decline markedly as students move up the age-grade ladder.

9. Difficulty in reaching out to a broad segment of the community and in sustaining participation. Involving working parents and single parents was often specifically mentioned as a problem.

10. Widespread perception among school administrators that family involvement is a kind of general public relations effort for the school system rather than a meaningful way of sharing educational accountability for the academic achievement of children.

The overall conclusion to be drawn from these findings is that parent involvement is still seen as a peripheral activity that has not been integrated into the main work of the schools. This essentially "PR" approach to parent involvement is precisely what alienates many parents and leads to charges among parent activists of school "manipulation" or "placation."[2]

It may be unwise to overgeneralize from the experience of one state. However, it should be pointed out that the local educational agencies selected for the Maryland study represent in many ways the diversity of the nation in microcosm. Rural areas, market cities dominating a rural hinterland, suburban areas, a central city, and areas undergoing rapid demographic change were included in the survey.

In fairness, it should be noted that the results of the Maryland study are scarcely surprising. Family involvement in education, keyed to raising children's achievement, is still at a "prescientific" stage of development. Local experimentation has provided a broad base of experience and practice, although it has also produced poorly documented efforts and the "reinvention of the wheel" on more than one occasion. It is our position that a sufficient data base exists to begin to place these efforts on a more systematic basis which could work a quiet revolution in our approach to education and substantially raise academic achievement.

ESTABLISHING PRIORITIES

Given the bewildering array of current programs and alternative modes of parent participation available, where do those concerned with increasing the effectiveness of schooling, whether they be policymakers, administrators, teachers, parents, or the lay public, begin? What are the basic premises and assumptions from which one can start to build meaningful parent involvement?

Our experience suggests, however, that priority attention should be given to developing the mode of participation which directly involves parents in the education of their own child. This is the basic, most fundamentally meaningful form of participation from which other modes can flow. It is often referred to as the "parent-as-tutor" approach.

The reasons for this position are twofold. First, it is the approach which a continuing line of research indicates is most directly linked to improved academic achievement. *Parent Involvement in Compensatory Education Programs* assessed the major models of parent involvement that evolved in the 1960s and found in general that the evidence supported participation of "parents-as-tutors" of their children.[3] In *Parents as Teachers of Young Children*, the more recent Stanford study, the authors state:

> As a group, the programs involving parents as teachers consistently produced significant immediate gains in children's IQ scores, and seemed to alter in a positive direction the teaching behavior of parents.[4]

The second reason for this position is that it offers the greatest opportunity for widespread involvement and sustained participation. Programs which require attendance at meetings or involvement in school activities during the day will necessarily have limited participation. The need to reach out to single parents and to families in which both parents work is a special concern. Furthermore, the parent-as-tutor approach appeals to the most basic parental motivation for involvement in the first place—the desire to help one's child do better in school.

Parents have generally turned to political activism and demands for shared control only when frustrated by what they perceive as a lack of responsiveness to their needs and concerns. Participation in advisory councils is difficult to maintain over the long term. Experience to date suggests that the creation of a political constituency, where none exists, will be a slow and time-consuming process. Many schools have found it difficult to identify willing candidates to serve on advisory councils and have undergone the frustration and embarrassment of poor turnout for community council elections.

The involvement of parents in the education of their own children means building a program as it should be built, from the bottom up, rather than from the top down. It creates a foundation of support and commitment for other kinds of involvement efforts. It may also obviate the need for many other kinds of public relations efforts as families begin to understand what is really involved in the education of children.

The parent-as-tutor model can be seen graphically in the "chains" described by Mimi Stearns. A "chain" of events is hypothesized beginning with involvement and leading to impact on student achievement. Stearns makes the following comments about the "chains":

> Describing the chains of events helps to clarify several fundamental issues and permits examination of specific linkages between parent involvement and child performance in school. Since the evidence currently available from the literature is equivocal, knowledge about specific links in the chain will have to be developed; such knowledge is probably the only way to explain why a given program of parent involvement may be successful while another program, which at least superficially resembles the first, has very different impacts. In addition, these descriptions permit us to look for evidence from additional sources such as the psychological literature of child development and small group theory. These chains, of course, do not take into account all the possibilities, and ... extensive research is still needed to confirm or challenge these sets of hypotheses.[5]

The effects of the parent-as-tutor model are:
1. Increased motivation of the child
2. Increased skills of the child
3. Improved self-image of the parent.

Stearns pictorially describes the chaining as shown in Figure 1.

Chain A	Chain B	Chain C
Child Motivation	Child Skill	Parent Self-Image

Parent learns how to teach own child

↓

Parent gives child individual attention and teaches new skills

↙ ↓ ↘

Child sees that parent perceives education as important

Parent perceives own new competence. Communicates confidence and fate control to child

↓ Child learns skills better ↓

Child is motivated to succeed in school

Child feels confident he/she can perform

↘ ↓ ↙

Child performs better on tests

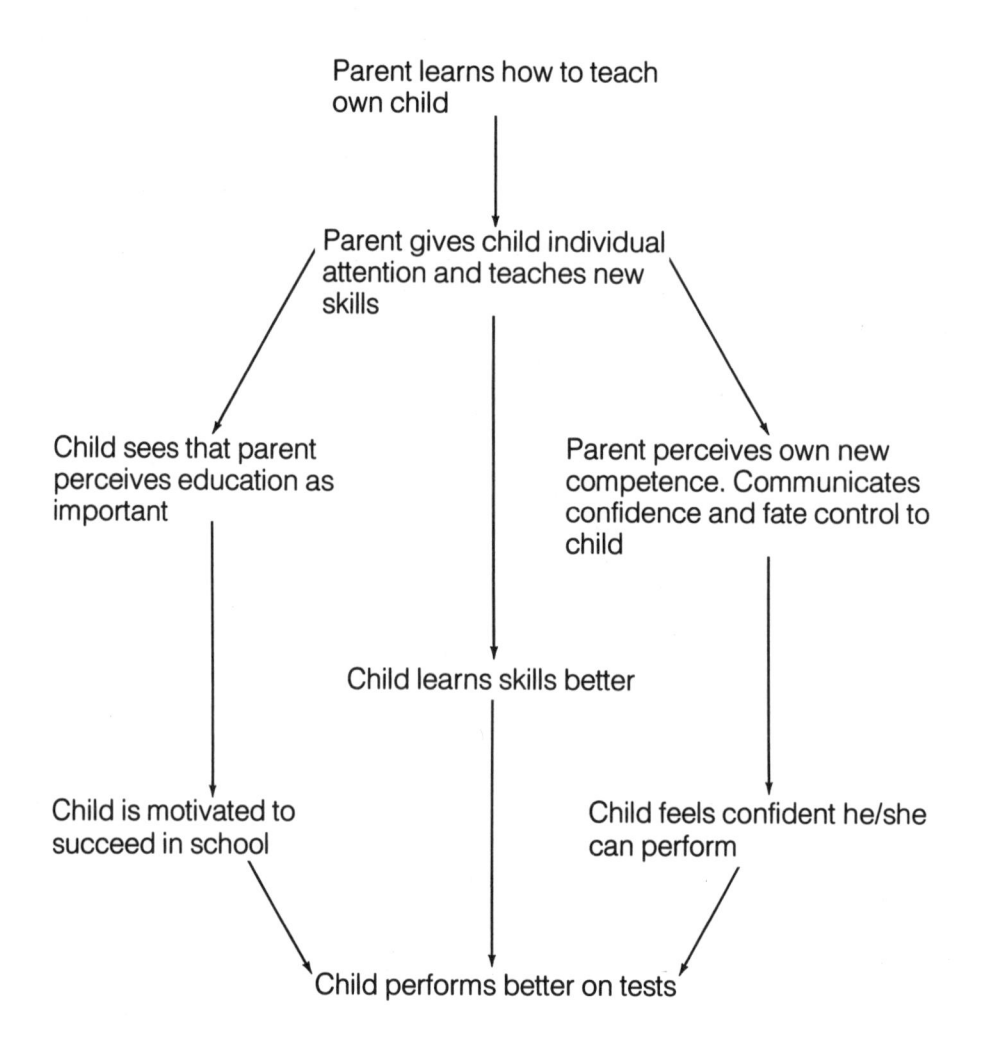

Figure 1. Parents as Learners and as Tutors of Their Own Children

The parent-as-tutor model does, however, pose the challenge of finding a low-cost, effective delivery system. Gordon's pioneering work at the preschool level involved the use of home visitors. While this approach is demonstrably effective, it is costly. This cost argues against its replication on a wide-scale basis, particularly when the schools are under today's budgetary pressures.

TRANSLATING THEORY INTO ACTION

The work of the Home and School Institute (HSI) has been devoted in large part to developing a parent-as-tutor strategy which can be utilized on a cost-effective basis with school-age children.

Basically, HSI has built programs based on assuming family strengths, not deficits. This nondeficit approach magnifies and builds on the strengths inherent in the family. It marshals available family resources and abilities to improve children's academic skills. This in turn increases self-esteem of family members and helps parents feel more secure in their parenting roles.

A deficit view of the family has served as a basis for a number of compensatory educational models. In Safran's analysis of the models outlined by Hess, it is assumed the low-income child has fewer meaningful experiences than the middle-class child.[6] Thus, the child's readiness for public school is diminished. A programmatic implication which grew out of this belief is that remediation can be applied which will assist the child in "catching up" to middle-class counterparts. Education for parents is visualized as filling in knowledge gaps. The experience to date suggests that compensatory programs built on this deficit view have not fulfilled original expectations.

The authors of a recent review of compensatory education efforts state:

> The cultural deprivation approach suggested that, because of limited life experience in the home, and a disintegrating family that speaks an inadequate language and lives in a poor community, the impoverished person is not able to achieve in school and ultimately cannot contribute to society. Children of the poor simply fall victim to the same conditions and sustain the cycle of poverty. In retrospect, it now seems that social scientists were naive to expect massive educational intervention to be a major force in interrupting the pov-

erty cycle. But many federally sponsored programs were based on this expectation. From the vantage point of the late 1970's a more pragmatic view of compensatory education may be possible.[7]

In contrast, the HSI nondeficit approach makes the following assumptions:

1. All children have had meaningful experiences. However, the disadvantaged child's experiences have been different and fewer in number in contributing to preparation for success in school.

2. Home environments, no matter how poor, are a citadel of care and concern for children.

3. All parents intrinsically possess the abilities to help their child succeed in school.

4. Family concern can be readily translated into practical support for children and for schools. Professionals need only to provide the materials and support to enable parents to become both more active and skilled participants in their child's education.

5. Schools should start with what the family has, instead of worrying about what it doesn't have.

6. Schools, no matter how understaffed or equipped, have the capabilities of reaching out and effecting parent involvement by using easy, inexpensive materials, without waiting for what probably won't come: organizational change or massive government funding.

The nondeficit approach constructs a mutually reinforcing home-school system. Families are assisted to:

1. Use strategies at home to supplement the school's work. The HSI parent involvement model is built on the basic premise of separate but complementary roles for parent and teacher.

2. Understand that accountability for a child's education can be shared, between school and home. Parents are helped in their role as key people in the student's learning process.

The parent is the most important teacher a child will ever have. Before a child can perform confidently within the classroom, he or she must have many positive and varied experiences with the family. If the primary supportive force in the child's life, the family, has respect for and confidence in his or her ability, the child will have self-respect and self-confidence.[8]

The parent-as-tutor model provides social reinforcement to the family in the form of increased attention, both to the parents from the school and from the parents to the child.

In the 1970s, Jesse Jackson's PUSH for Excellence program endeavored to raise the self-esteem of minority students by promoting the positive image that success is within their grasp. As a practical result, thousands of parents and children signed agreements with schools promising to make sure that their children do their homework—with the television off. This has focused attention on one strategy parents can use to assist the schools. But, PUSH asked parents to play a rather limited role; parents are able to play a far more active role, building on and going beyond the school to enhance their children's interests and achievement. Clearly, additional involvement strategies need to be developed within a programmatic structure.

One of the strategies we at the Home and School Institute have developed is called "Home Learning Recipes." The recipes are specific, practical, no-cost activities for learning at home. Their goal is to build family interaction and children's academic achievement without duplicating the work of the school.

Since 1965, when the HSI parent programs began, Home Learning Recipes have been prepared and tested in homes with children ranging from kindergarten through the secondary grades. The recipe format outlines on one page, at a glance, activity objectives, evaluation, and adaptations, in easy-to-read, easy-to-do activities. The difference between HSI Home Learning and typical schoolwork is that HSI activities are designed to use the resources of the home and the community. They are not typical schoolwork, even though they concentrate on the basic 3R skills.

Research conducted by one of the authors was the first major test of "Home Learning Recipes." Four classes of first grade children from both inner-city and suburban schools were given these home-based activities designed to supplement but not duplicate schoolwork in the basic skills areas. The children carrying these single sheets of paper home did the activities with their parents. The recipes used simple everyday household items. After a series of eight biweekly recipe treatments, the children's reading levels were improved at a statistically significant level.[9]

The basic HSI recipe approach has been replicated and adapted for use in a number of settings. In *Project HELP* in Benton Harbor, Michigan, the recipes model was used in a citywide Title I program for first graders. A cost effectiveness study indicated that gains per pupil were achieved for $4.31 per child, compared with "pull out" special class instructional costs of $565 per child per year.[10] In *Project AHEAD* (Accelerating Home Education and Development) in Los Angeles under the sponsorship of the Southern Christian Leadership Conference West, CETA workers were trained successfully to help families, most of whom are Black or Hispanic, to teach their children at home using the recipe approach.[11]

In "Families Learning Together," funded by the Charles Stewart Mott Foundation, recipes were designed and field-tested which simultaneously provide parents with information in areas such as health and safety, consumer education, and family relationships while the parents in turn work with their children in reading and mathematics.[12]

The "Home Learning Recipe" approach is a double-tiered, impact model melding the child's academic achievement, parents' and child's feelings of self-esteem, and a modeling of parent behavior supporting the value of education. Basically, all of these programs combine the parent-as-tutor model with the nondeficit approach.

Data from these projects indicate that additional benefits accompany a nondeficit approach to the parent-as-tutor model. Beyond those identified by Stearns, the following effects can also be expected:

Increased motivational skills of parents to work with their child

Increased parenting skills and understanding of the school's role

Increased interaction between parent and child.

Over the years, HSI has developed a bank of recipes in the basic skills areas so that it is possible to choose among a variety of activities to fit the needs and interests of a particular child or group of children without extensive teacher involvement in the design of the materials. The approach is self-teaching and perpetuating in that it is relatively easy, once the basic technique is mastered, for teachers and parents to continue to create recipes and learning activities on their own. The approach can function on an individualized diagnostic-prescriptive level with the selection and/or design of recipes to meet the particular developmental or remedial needs of each child. Recipes have been used successfully with bilingual and also with handicapped populations. Perhaps most important is the finding that families do these activities with their children, voluntarily and delightedly, pleased with themselves as teachers and pleased with their children as learners.

BUILDING AN EFFECTIVE PROGRAM

The school is *the* social institution that has contact with students over many years. This fact alone gives schools both the opportunity and the responsibility to reach out to the student and the family beyond the classroom walls.

In a study of Atlanta's attempt to implement *A Plan for Improvement*, Whitaker observes that "School personnel must assume initiative for developing a working partnership between community and school."[13]

This is not easy. But, beginning steps need to and can be taken. To help educators more clearly define and assume this commitment, we have identified the general elements or characteristics of successful school-family programs.

The following seven characteristics can serve as criteria for developing any school system's program:

1. Parent participation is most widespread and sustained when parents view their participation as *directly* linked to the achievement of their children. Developing and maintaining a high level of parent participation is a problem for many programs. An important, intrinsic reward and reinforcement for parents is the success experienced by their own children.

2. Parent/community involvement programs need to include the opportunity for families to supplement and reinforce the development of academic skills with work in the home. Home involvement also offers the possibility of participation to people who cannot attend in-school meetings.

3. Involvement programs should provide for various modes of participation. There is a particular need to reach out to parents with alternative participatory modes, in addition to existing advisory councils and volunteer programs. This is especially needed by

single parents and families with both parents working.

4. Involvement opportunities need to exist at *all* levels of schooling. Though research and school-community program development thus far have centered on the early childhood years, continuing support and reinforcement are needed as the child moves through school. A particular need for programs exists in the middle and junior high adolescent years.

5. The impetus for parent/community involvement so far appears to emerge from federally funded and other special programs of a compensatory nature. Opportunities and resources for these target populations are often greater than those available to parents of the community in general. Strategies that involve the whole community ensure broader support for an integration of these special programs into the total school procedures.

6. Parent/community involvement programs are more effective if active support and cooperation is gained from school boards, community agencies, and professional organizations.

7. Parent-community involvement needs to be viewed as a legitimate activity of the schools and as an *integral* part of its delivery of services, not an add-on. *Reaching the family is as important as reaching the child.*[14]

In order to build programs to meet these criteria, each part of the educational network must perform certain essential roles. The authors have compiled a listing of the major tasks that need to be carried out to do the job. These are identified by the roles in the educational hierarchy.

What Can a State Department of Education Do?

State departments are in an excellent position to help school districts begin to mobilize parent and community support and resources. Here are some ways:

• Assist in reorientation of thinking about the importance of parent-community involvement in the total education process.

Help school districts delineate goals and commit resources of time, money, and people to implement and evaluate home/school programs in a systematic and meaningful way.

- Identify and support school-family involvement as an integral part of instructional services.

Encourage local educational agencies to develop a clearly defined philosophy of the home/school educational partnership which can serve as the basis for the development of specific policies, guidelines, and practices.

- Advise LEA's about program operations encompassing research, development, dissemination, and technical assistance.

Highlight programs and practices for statewide attention. Provide mechanisms for sharing home/school partnership programs at statewide and regional meetings.

Build outreach from schools to community agencies by preparing and distributing a handbook to each LEA detailing the services available to families through community agencies.

Establish an information bank for resources, promising program practices and approaches as a resource for local educational agencies.

Serve as a clearinghouse to promote the increased sharing of information among LEA's and community agencies within the state. It was found in the HSI/State of Maryland survey that community agencies offer a broad network of services to families which are not yet being utilized by the schools.

What Can Local School Boards and School Superintendents Do?

- Build awareness of and provide training to board members and personnel, as needed, for school-family involvement: provide leadership techniques and strategies for developing materials, practices, and programs.

Focus attention on the role of the superintendent's staff to plan and coordinate the home/school programs: one way to do this is to fund one position with this specific responsibility.

Examine successful home/school practices within federally funded programs to be replicated on a cost effective basis within other schools in the LEA.

- Assist school personnel in accepting and using all and any additional home and community resources to supplement the school's role.

Help to maintain close working relations between citizens and school officials in the development of school policies, goals, priorities, and programs.

Institute selection processes for advisory councils to assure wider community participation.

Establish a hierarchy of Citizens' Advisory Councils beginning at the local school level and proceeding to the district level with clearly defined tasks and responsibilities.

Develop and encourage additional modes of family/community participation beyond the advisory council.

What Can Principals Do?

- Raise consciousness about the home and community as the key to student achievement: publicize and support ideas, materials, and strategies that promote this belief.
- Learn about and replicate promising practices of other schools within one's own school.

Adapt successful program practices from the preschool and elementary levels to the needs of older students and their families.

- Set up a functional design for operating a parent advisory council at the school: combine specific tasks and advisory functions as a focus for positive parental efforts.

Project for parents a realistic picture of what schools can accomplish.

What Can Teachers Do?

- Recognize that all parents are a significant force in their child's education. Search for ways to involve parents as educational partners.

Use the resources of the home for materials, ideas, and as resources for different subject areas.

Teach parents how they can help their children at home: provide home learning tips on how to supplement the work of the school.

Utilize effectively the contribution of parents' skills, insights, talents, and concerns to the educational process.

Show parents in a variety of ways that you care for them and their child: Inform parents of what's happening at school on a regular basis; offer a variety of school-parent programs and materials designed to build the home/school/community educational partnership. Include special events and meetings with a teaching purpose. Schedule some programs away from the school setting. Include ways to reach working parents and single parents. Set up as many father-oriented events as possible.

Encourage parents to visit the school, to confer on a regular basis, and to use the school as a source for help and referral to community agencies.

LEADERSHIP FOR CHANGE

Working on a partnership basis with the home is more difficult today than it might have been a few years ago. Existing patterns of neighborhood schools have changed. Reaching out to parents is not always a down-the-block contact. It's often a matter of many miles. Conferences are harder to set up. Other ways will have to be employed to reach, inform, and receive advice from parents in addition to the traditional face-to-face meeting.

Parents have needs that schools will have to meet. After years of being told that they don't know "the right way" to teach, parents may need to have their confidence restored. Schools have to convince parents to trust themselves and once again regard themselves as their child's primary and ongoing teachers.

The caring, the improved education, and the increased leisure time of parents offer great potential for building a home-school educational partnershp. A growing number of parents want to know how they can best help their children educationally.

Reaching out to those parents who are ready to help will make the school's work easier, not harder. It's not doubling the burden of the school's job; it's lessening it by sharing accountability with the people identified by research as those able to make significant educational impact. The healthy skepticism and caring now shown by a growing number of parents offer hope for school personnel today. Not even the best school can do the job alone.

Educators seeking substantive family involvement in education need to be prepared to exert leadership—with staff and with parents. Working with families requires certain basic attitudes, skills, and behaviors.

Instead of starting with "what do we have to fix?" educators need to start with "what can we build on?" The professional orientation changes from focusing on the family's deficits to building on the family's strengths.

Educators will have to learn to work effectively with adults, which may require new skills. Teachers need to know and be able to impart to parents an overview of the research that supports the parent-as-teacher approach. Teachers need skills as leaders and as problem solvers. More specifically, they may need help in running better conferences and meetings and teachers need to know how to develop and use materials for outreach to the home. The focus is not just on the child but on the family as new "home-style" teachers of the child.

Teachers need to be able to build partnerships with the home, in an orderly, noncrisis fashion. The emphasis must be on prevention before issues become problems. The emphasis must be on children's abilities, before they become disabilities. The emphasis must be on what can be done with what is available now!

Programs can begin with one parent, one teacher, one school, one community. The goal is clearly defined. The strategies can be directly charted. Let us begin. Let us continue.

FOOTNOTES

[1] Home and School Institute. *Survey of Home/School/Community Programs and Practices in the State of Maryland*. Report submitted to the Maryland State Department of Education, October 1978.
[2] Sherry Arnstein. "Eight Rungs on the Ladder of Citizen Participation." In: Edgar Colin and Barry Passett, editors. *Citizen Participation: Effecting Community Change*. New York: Praeger, 1971.
[3] Stanford Research Institute. *Parent Involvement in Compensatory Education Programs*. Washington, D.C.: Office of Planning, Budgeting, and Evaluation, U.S. Office of Education, 1973.
[4] Barbara Goodson and Robert Hess. *Parents as Teachers of Young Children: An Evaluative Review of Some Comtemporary Concepts and Programs*. Palo Alto, Calif.: Stanford University, 1975.
[5] Mimi Stearns and others. *Parent Involvement in Compensatory Education Programs*. Menlo Park, Calif.: Stanford Research Institute, August 1973. pp. 29–49, as quoted by

Daniel Safran. "Evaluating Parent Involvement." Oakland, Calif.: Center for Study of Parent Involvement, January 1974. pp. 7, 9.

[6]Safran, *op. cit.*, p. 3.

[7]Karen Hill-Scott and J. Eugene Grigsby. "Some Policy Recommendations for Compensatory Education." *Phi Delta Kappan* 60 (6): 443–46; February 1979.

[8]William W. Purkey. *Self-Concept and School Achievement.* Englewood Cliffs, N.J.: Prentice-Hall, 1970. p. 2.

[9]Dorothy Rich. "The Relationship of the Home Learning Lab Technique to First Grade Student Achievement." Doctoral dissertation, Catholic University of America, Washington, D.C., 1976.

[10]Gladys E. Burks. "An Analysis of the Cost-Effectiveness of Title I Pull-Out Instruction in the Benton Harbor Area Schools." Benton Harbor, Michigan, Schools, May 1978.

[11]Bernard Plaskett. *AHEAD Report.* Los Angeles: Southern Christian Leadership Conference/West, September 1978.

[12]Home and School Institute. *Families Learning Together.* Washington, D.C.: HSI, 1978–79.

[13]Barbara Ingram Whitaker. "Citizen Participation in Educational Decision Making in an Urban School District as Perceived by Parents and Administrators." Doctoral dissertation, Georgia State University, 1977.

[14]Home and School Institute. *Survey of Home/School/Community Programs, op. cit.*

APPENDIX B. REFERENCES AND REPORTS ON PARENT INVOLVEMENT

STUDIES OF FAMILIES AS EDUCATORS: 1979-86

Supported by the National Institute of Education and
the Office of Educational Research and Improvement,
U.S. Department of Education

The following reports were supported by the above agencies. During the period 1979-82 a Families as Educators team in the NIE, led by Oliver Moles, sponsored a number of these studies. Others were funded by other units of NIE, and later by OERI, which succeeded NIE in 1985.

This listing covers various aspects of families as educators. The topics include:

- overviews
- home-school relationships
- attitudes toward parent involvement
- family educational processes
- literacy development in the family
- parent education/family support
- home uses of television
- single parents
- working parents

Several of the laboratories and centers supported by NIE and OERI have devoted programs of studies to aspects of families as educators. The reports from these organizations are rather extensive, and are listed separately. They are cross-referenced where appropriate.

Please note the following codes beside the reports:

Report is available from OERI
**Abstract* of report is available from OERI

For other reports, consult the cited journal or book, or the organization which produced the report.

For those available from OERI please contact:
> Oliver Moles
> Office of Research, OERI
> U.S. Department of Education
> 555 New Jersey Avenue, N.W.
> Washington, D.C. 20208
> (202) 357-6207

Family Educational Processes

**Fenster, E. (1982). College attendance by working adults and its effects on the educational motivations of their children. Detroit: To Educate the People Consortium, Wayne State University.

**Leichter, H. J., and others. (1982). An examination of cognitive processes in everyday family life. New York: Elbenwood Center for the Study of the Family as Educator, Teachers College, Columbia University.

**Levenstein, P., and O'Hara, J. M. (1982). Tracing the parent-child network: A research project. Garden City, NY: The Verbal Interaction Project, Inc., Adelphi University.

Literacy Development in the Family

**Anderson, A. B. (1982). School age final report. San Diego: Laboratory of Comparative Human Cognition, University of California, San Diego.

**Chall, J., and Snow, C. (1982). Families and literacy: The contribution of out-of-school experiences to children's acquisition of literacy. Cambridge, MA: Harvard Graduate School of Education.

*Hess, R. D., and Holloway, S. (1979). The intergenerational transmission of literacy. Palo Alto, CA: Stanford University.

**Leichter, H. J., and others (1981). The family's role in the acquisition of literacy for learning. Vol. I and Vol. II - Appendices. New York: Elbenwood Center for the Study of the Family as Educator, Teachers College, Columbia University.

Parent Education/Family Support

*Chilman, C. S. (1979). A brief history of parent education in the United States. Milwaukee: School of Social Welfare, University of Wisconsin-Milwaukee.

*Cochran, M. (1982). Family Matters update: Design, baseline findings, policy implications and program developments from a family support study. Ithaca, NY: Cornell University.

*Cochran, M., and Henderson, C. R., Jr., eds. (1982). The ecology of urban family life: A summary report to the National Institute of Education. Ithaca, NY: The Comparative Ecology of Human Development Project, Cornell University.

*Cochran, M., and Henderson, C. R., Jr. (1985). Family Matters: Evaluation of the parental empowerment program. Ithaca, NY: The Comparative Ecology of Human Development Project, Cornell University.

*Cochran, M., and Henderson, C. R., Jr. (1986). Family Matters: Evaluation of the parental empowerment program. A summary of the final report. Ithaca, NY: The Comparative Ecology of Human Development Project, Cornell University.

*Haskins, R. (1981). Parent education and public policy: A Conference report. Chapel Hill, NC: Bush Institute for Child and Family Policy, University of North Carolina at Chapel Hill.

*Haskins, R., and Adams, D., eds. (1983). *Parent education and public policy*. Norwood, NJ: Ablex Publishing Corporation.

Longtain, M. J. (1981, Feb.). Executive summary: Parent models of child socialization. Austin, TX: Southwest Educational Development Laboratory.

Williams, D. L., Jr. (1981, April). Executive summary of the final report: Assessing parent education program relevance to changing family structures. Austin, TX: Southwest Educational Development Laboratory.

Home Uses of Television

*Corder-Bolz, C. R. (1981). Family educational uses of television. Austin, TX: Southwest Educational Development Laboratory.

*Corder-Bolz, C. R. (1981). Evaluation of eight methodologies for study of family use of television. Austin, TX: Southwest Educational Development Laboratory.

Gotts, E. E. (1980). Long-term effects of a home-oriented pre-school program. *Childhood Education*, Feb./Mar. 1980, 228-234.

Single Parents

**Hetherington, E. M., Camara, K. A., and Featherman, D. L. (1981). Cognitive performance, school behavior and achievement of children from one-parent households.

*Moles, O. C. (1982). Trends in divorce and effects on children. Paper presented at the Meetings of the American Academy for the Advancement of Science.

Working Parents

Hayes, C. D., and Kamerman, S. B., eds. (1983). *Working parents: Experiences and Outcomes*. Washington, DC: National Academy Press.

**Hoffman, L. W. (1980). The effects of maternal employment on the academic attitudes and performance of school-aged children. Ann Arbor: The University of Michigan.

Kamerman, S. B., and Hayes, C. D., eds. (1982). *Families that work: Children in a changing world*. Washington, DC: National Academy Press.

APPALACHIA EDUCATIONAL LABORATORY*

Selected References on Parent Involvement: 1980-86

Gotts, E. E. (1980). Long-term effects on a home-oriented pre-school program. *Childhood Education*, Feb./March 1980, 228-234.

Gotts, E. E. (1983). Home-school communications and parent involvement. Charleston, WV: Appalachia Educational Laboratory, Inc.

Gotts, E. E. (1984). Communicating through the home-school handbook: Guidelines for principals. Charleston, WV: Appalachia Educational Laboratory, Inc.

---

*For further information contact: Publications Office, Appalachia Educational Laboratory, Inc., P.O. Box 1348, Charleston, WV 25325. The telephone number is (304) 347-0400.

Gotts, E. E. (1984). Communicating through newsletters in secondary schools. Charleston, WV: Appalachia Educational Laboratory, Inc.

Gotts, E. E. (1984, April). School-home communications at the secondary level. Paper presented at American Educational Research Association, Montreal.

Gotts, E. E., and Purnell, R. F. (1984, June). Appalachian parents' views of home-school relations at the secondary level. Paper presented at the Fifth Annual Conference on Appalachian Children and Families, Morehead State University, Kentucky.

Gotts, E. E., and Purnell, R. F. (1984). "The Modern Dilemma of School-Home Communications." Charleston, WV: Appalachia Educational Laboratory, Inc.

Gotts, E. E., and Purnell, R. F. (1985). *Improving home-school communications*. Fastback 230. Bloomington, IN: Phi Delta Kappa Educational Foundation.

Gotts, E. E., and Purnell, R. F. (In press). Communications: Key to school-home relations. In Lezotte, L. E., Boger, R. P., Griffore, R. J., eds. *Child rearing in the home and school*. New York: Plenum.

Gotts, E. E., and Sattes, B. (1982). Interviews and coding procedures for assessing school-family communications. Charleston, WV: Appalachia Educational Laboratory, Inc.

McAffe, O. (1985). A resources notebook for improving school-home communications. Charleston, WV: Appalachia Educational Laboratory.

Spriggs, A. M. (1984, Jan.). School personnel training for working with families. Paper presented at the 1984 Annual Meeting of the Association of Teacher Educators. New Orleans, LA.

CENTER FOR RESEARCH ON ELEMENTARY AND MIDDLE SCHOOLS*

List of Reports on Parent Involvement

I. *Teachers' Practices of Parent Involvement*

Parent Involvement: A Survey of Teacher Practices.
Henry Jay Becker and Joyce L. Epstein.
Elementary School Journal, November 1982, *83,* 85-102. (P-11   Reprint $.90)

Influence on Teachers' Use of Parent Involvement.
Henry Jay Becker and Joyce L. Epstein.
Report 324, The Johns Hopkins University, Center for Social Organization of Schools, 1982. (P-12   Report $2.05)

Teacher Practices of Parent Involvement: Problems and Possibilities.
Joyce L. Epstein and Henry Jay Becker.
Elementary School Journal, November 1982, *83,* 103-113. (P-13   Reprint $.55)

II. *Students' Reactions to Parent Involvement*

Student Reactions to Teacher Practices of Parent Involvement.
Joyce L. Epstein.
Paper presented at the annual meeting of the American Educational Research Association, 1982. (P-21   Report $1.05)

Effects of Parent Involvement on Change in Student Achievement in Reading and Math.
Joyce L. Epstein.
In *Literacy Through Family, Community, and School Interaction.* S. Silvern, ed., Greenwich, CT: JAI Press, forthcoming. (P-22   Report $.90)

III. *Parents' Reactions to Parent Involvement*

Parents' Reactions to Teacher Practices of Parent Involvement.
Joyce L. Epstein.

---

*For reprints of articles, Center reports, or information contact: Dr. Joyce L. Epstein, Schools and Families Project, The Johns Hopkins University, Center for Research on Elementary and Middle Schools (CREMS), 3505 N. Charles Street, Baltimore, MD 21218. (301-338-7570)

Elementary School Journal, January 1986, *86,* 277-294. (P-31   Reprints $.90)

School Policy and Parent Involvement: Research Results.
Joyce L. Epstein.
Educational Horizons, Winter 1984, *62,* 70-72. (P-32   Reprint $.15)

Single Parents and The Schools: The Effect of Marital Status on Parent and Teacher Evaluations.
Joyce L. Epstein.
Report 353, The Johns Hopkins University, Center for Social Organization of Schools, 1984. (P-33   Report $3.00)

IV. *Other Issues Related to Parent Involvement*

Homework Practices, Achievements, and Behaviors of Elementary School Students.
Joyce L. Epstein.
Paper presented at the annual meeting of the American Sociological Association, 1985. (P-41   Report $1.20)

A Question of Merit: Principals' and Parents' Evaluations of Teachers.
Joyce L. Epstein.
Educational Researcher, 1985, *14* (7), 3-10. (P-42   Reprint $.40)

Home and School Connections in Schools of the Future: Implications of Research on Parent Involvement.
Joyce L. Epstein.
Peabody Journal of Education, 1985, *62,* 18-41. (P-43   Reprint $.60)

Parent-Teacher Conferences
Joyce L. Esptein.
Article to appear in *Encyclopedia of School Administration and Supervision,* in press. (P-44   Report $.30)

V. *Summaries of Research on Parent Involvement*

Testimony before the Prevention Strategies Task Force of the Select Subcommittee on Children, Youth, and Families.
Joyce L. Epstein.
In *Improving American Education: Roles for Parents,* June 7, 1984, Washington, D.C.: Government Printing Office. (P-51   Reprint $.40)

When School and Family Partnerships Work: Implications for Changing the Role of Teachers.
Joyce L. Epstein.
Paper presented at the annual meeting of the American Educational Research Association, 1985. (P-52   Report $.60)

Parent Involvement: What Research Says to Administrators.
Joyce L. Epstein.
Education in Urban Society, in press. (P-53   Report $1.20)

Parent Involvement (Five types of parent involvement programs).
Joyce L. Epstein.
Article to appear in *Encyclopedia of School Administration and Supervision,* in press. (P-54   Report $.55)

Parent Involvement: Implications for Limited-English-Proficient Parents.
Joyce L. Epstein.
Proceedings of the Symposium on Issues of Parent Involvement and Literacy.
Trinity College, Department of Education and Counseling, 1986. (P-55   Reprint $.50)

VI. *Research and Development: Processes and Prototypic Activities*

(For teachers' evaluations and cooperative research studies.)

Tying Research to Practice. TIPS: Teachers Involve Parents in Schoolwork.
Joyce L. Epstein.
Paper presented at the annual meeting of the American Educational Research Association, 1985. (P-61   Report $1.80)

Teachers' Manual: Teachers Involve Parents in Schoolwork (TIPS)
Joyce L. Epstein.
Manual for introducing the TIPS process and building parent involvement programs. (P-62   Report $3.65)
Available on request from author:
TIPS Process and Activities in Math, Grades 1-4.
TIPS Process and Activities in Science, Grades 2-5.

VII. *Theoretical Perspectives on Family and School Organizations and Their Connections*

Family Structures and Student Motivation: A Developmental Perspective.

Joyce L. Epstein.
In C. Ames and R. Ames, eds. Research on Motivation in Education (vol. 3). New York: Academic Press (in press). (P-71 Report available in mimeo, $2.50)

Toward a Theory of Family-School Connections.
Joyce L. Epstein.
Baltimore: The Johns Hopkins University Center for Research on Elementary and Middle Schools. CREMS REPORT 3. (P-73 Report $3.00)

Please add $1.00 for library rate postage and handling.

SOUTHWEST EDUCATIONAL DEVELOPMENT LABORATORY*

Selected References on Parent Involvement

Chavkin, N. F., and Garza-Lubeck, M. (1987, in press). *A resource directory for training educators for parent involvement.* Austin, TX: Southwest Educational Development Laboratory.

Chavkin, N. F., and Williams, D. L., Jr. (1985). Parent involvement in education. *(School Social Work Journal,* 10: 35-46.

Chavkin, N. F., and Williams, D. L., Jr. (1985, November). Executive summary of the final report: Parent involvement in education project. Austin, TX: Southwest Educational Development Laboratory.

Chavkin, N. F., and Williams, D. L., Jr. (1987, in press). Enhancing parent involvement: Guidelines for access to an important resource for school administrators. *Education and Urban Society,* forthcoming, February 1987.

Corder-Bolz, C. R. (1981). Family educational use of television. Austin, TX: Southwest Educational Development Laboratory.

Corder-Bolz, C. R. (1981). Evaluation of eight methodologies for study of family use of television. Austin, TX: Southwest Educational Development Laboratory.

---

*For further information contact: Publications office, Southwest Educational Development Laboratory, 211 East 7th Street, Austin, TX 78701. (512) 476-6861.

Espinoza, R., and Naron, N. (1983, December). Work and family life among Anglo, Black and Mexican American single-parent families: Executive summary of the 1983 annual report. Austin, TX: Southwest Educational Development Laboratory. ($1.75).

Longtain, M. J. (1981, February). Executive summary: Parent models of child socialization. Austin, TX: Southwest Educational Development Laboratory. ($1.50).

Mason, T., and Espinoza, R. (1983, January). Executive summary of the final report: Working parents project. Austin, TX: Southwest Educational Development Laboratory. ($1.75).

Stallworth, J. T. (1981, April). Executive summary of the final report: A survey of teacher educators on parent involvement in schools. Austin, TX: Southwest Educational Development Laboratory. ($1.50).

Stallworth, J. T. (1982, February). Parent involvement at the elementary school level: A survey of teachers (Executive summary). Austin, TX: Southwest Educational Development Laboratory. ($1.75).

Stallworth, J. T., and Williams, D. L., Jr. (1982). A survey of parents regarding parent involvement in schools (Executive summary). Austin, TX: Southwest Educational Development Laboratory. ($1.75). ERIC ED 225 682.

Stallworth, J. T., and Williams, D. L., Jr. (1983). A survey of school administrators and policymakers (Executive summary). Austin, TX: Southwest Educational Development Laboratory. ($1.00).

Williams, D. L., Jr. (1981). *Research to improve family and school life*. Austin, TX: Southwest Educational Development Laboratory. ($6.00).

Williams, D. L., Jr. (1981, April). Executive summary of the final report: Assessing parent education program relevance to changing family structures. Austin, TX: Southwest Educational Development Laboratory.

Williams, D. L., Jr. (1982). Parent involvement at the elementary school level: A survey of principals (Executive summary). Austin, TX: Southwest Educational Development Laboratory. ($1.75).

Williams, D. L., Jr. (1983, May 12). Educator and parent perspectives on parent involvement: Implications for strengthening families and schools. Paper presented at the sixth National Symposium for Building Family Strengths.

Williams, D. L., Jr. (1984). Parent involvement in education: Some conclusions and recommendations. Austin, TX: Southwest Educational Development Laboratory.

Williams, D. L., Jr. (1984). *Proceedings of a working conference on parent involvement and teacher training: Recommendations for developing guidelines and strategies for training elementary school teachers for parent involvement.* Austin, TX: Southwest Educational Development Laboratory. ($3.25).

Williams, D. L., Jr., and Chavkin, N. F. (1986). Teacher/parent partnerships: Guidelines and strategies for training teachers about parent involvement (Executive summary). Austin, TX: Southwest Educational Development Laboratory.

Williams, D. L., Jr., and Chavkin, N. F. (1986). Teacher/parent partnerships: Guidelines and strategies for training teachers in parent involvement skills. Austin, TX: Southwest Educational Development Laboratory. ($3.00) ERIC ED 255 289.

Williams, D. L., Jr., and Chavkin, N. F. (1986). Strengthening parent involvement. *National Association of Elementary School Principals' Streamlined Seminar,* 4: 1-4.

SYNTHESIS OF RECENT RESEARCH ON PARENT PARTICIPATION IN CHILDREN'S EDUCATION*

by Oliver C. Moles

Among educators, there is considerable interest in parent involvement in education. In an NEA poll (1981), over 90 percent of teachers in all parts of the country and at all grade levels stated that more home-school interaction would be desirable.

The nationwide Gallup polls of public attitudes toward education reflect a similar interest, as well as approval of some specific forms of parent participation. When asked what more the public schools should be doing, a frequent suggestion was for closer teacher-parent relationships, including more conferences and information on what parents can do at home to help children in school. Eighty percent of parents with school-age children agreed with the idea of parents attending school one evening a month to learn how to improve children's behavior and interest in school work (Gallup, 1978).

Reviewing survey findings over a ten-year period, Gallup (1978) concluded: "A joint and coordinated effort by parents and teachers is essential to dealing more successfully with problems of discipline, motivation, and the development of good work habits at home and in school.... For little added expense (which the public is willing to pay) the public schools can, by working with parents, meet educational standards impossible to reach without such cooperation."

The idea of parents assisting their children's education by working with schools has been the subject of much debate. On the one hand is the interest of educators and parents and evidence of the idea's usefulness, and on the other hand are serious barriers to its implementation. Nevertheless, individual teachers, schools, and school systems have developed programs and practices to involve parents in their children's schooling. I would like to describe examples of some recent studies, including programs in the upper grades, and draw conclusions that may help others contemplating similar activities.

---

*From *Educational Leadership* (November 1982), pp. 44-47. Copyright © 1982 by the Association for Supervision and Curriculum Development. Reprinted with permission of the Association for Supervision and Curriculum Development. All rights reserved.

SOME EFFECTS OF PARENT PARTICIPATION ON ACHIEVEMENT

At the preschool level, there is much support for parent involvement. Bronfenbrenner (1974), who has reviewed a variety of early intervention programs, concluded that the active involvement of the family is critical to program success. It reinforces and helps sustain the effects of school programs.

At the elementary level, a number of studies also point to benefits of parent involvement (Phi Delta Kappa, 1980). In a recent review of related studies, Henderson (1981) stated: "Taken together, what is most interesting about the research is that it all points in the same direction. The form of parent involvement does not seem to be critical, so long as it is reasonably well-planned, comprehensive, and long-lasting."

However, some studies of parents' home participation to aid school learning suggest that effects are not universally positive. In a study of Michigan elementary schools, Brookover and his associates (1979) found greater parental involvement in white than in black schools, but only in black schools was high involvement associated with greater achievement.

A recent large study of parent involvement in ESEA Title I, the ESEA Title VII Bilingual Program, Follow Through, and the Emergency School Aid Act presents a cautious picture of parent participation activities. After advisory groups, the next most common form of involvement was communication, mostly from the project to the home. While most projects provided some kind of parent education, usually on a one-time basis, few helped parents teach their own children at home or had arranged face-to-face discussions between parents and staff members (Burns, 1982). Thus, even in large federally funded programs there was little sustained effort to communicate with parents and help them assist in the instructional process.

These studies suggest that there is much still to be learned about the kinds of families and schools, and the kinds of home-school and parent-child relationships, that promote student achievement. Nevertheless, there is reason for optimism. As Benson (1980) observed, "No group of parents, hence, should regard their efforts toward their children as foreordained to failure."

HOW PARENTS PARTICIPATE

Typically, parent participation consists of at least two distinctive stages and under the best conditions implies an equality between parents and school personnel. First are the parent-school contacts in which parents learn about their children's school performance and ways they can assist. These contacts also help teachers learn of student capabilities and interests and about parents' ability to help their children. Second are the home learning activities themselves in which children acquire information and skills useful for the classroom.

Parent-school contacts may take the form of notes, conferences, home visits, and joint participation in workshops and classes. Children become home learners through at least four kinds of educational processes: home instruction, enrichment activities, contracts to supervise homework or provide incentives for good work, and modeling of educational pursuits by family members.

Various kinds of parent involvement were evaluated by elementary teachers in a six-state regional survey (Williams, 1981). Generally, teachers were not enthusiastic about parent participation in curriculum development, instruction, or school governance. They did support other forms of parent involvement, such as assisting with homework or tutoring children, but felt that teachers should give parents ideas about how to help. Teachers noted that their own schools did not usually provide opportunities for parents and teachers to work together on such activities.

A companion survey of elementary principals in the same six states produced similar results (Williams, 1981). Principals valued parent participation in children's home learning for several reasons: it helps schools, reinforces school learning, and is within parents' capabilities. But the principals also felt that parents lack adequate training to prepare them for an active role in children's home learning.

BARRIERS TO HOME-SCHOOL COLLABORATION

A variety of conditions may limit the extent of home-school communication and parent cooperation with schools. For example, many parents face competing demands of work and family life, come from different cultural backgrounds, and feel mistrust and anxiety when dealing with school staff. For their part, many teachers also face competing demands at school and at home, lack training for dealing with parents, and may have difficulty relating to culturally different families.

Lightfoot (1978) goes a step farther and suggests that home-school relations are inherently in conflict. She believes that different priorities and perceptions of families and schools, such as concern for one's own child versus responsibility for group progress, will inevitably create conflict over the means of attaining common goals. She sees collaboration largely as a one-way process with schools seldom accommodating in a significant way to family needs.

In their exploratory study of home-school collaboration in two inner-city junior high schools, Tangri and Leitch (1982) identified a number of barriers. Because this study deals with families of older students, about whom less is known regarding home-school relationships, it is of special interest. Teachers reported competing home responsibilities, fears for their own safety at evening events, the perception that parents do not transmit educational values, feeling overwhelmed by the problems of their students and families, and low expectations regarding parents' follow-up efforts. Parents also reported a number of barriers including family health problems, work schedules, having small children, receiving only "bad news" from school, fears for their safety, late notice of meetings, and not understanding their children's homework.

Both parents and teachers recognized that most communication between them was negative—teacher messages about poor student performance and parent complaints regarding events in school. Both groups also reported that the school work was beyond the comprehension of some parents, despite the desire of many to understand. Both parents and teachers suggested workshops for parents interested in becoming familiar with course assignments (Tangri and Leitch, 1982).

Despite such barriers, some programs and practices are adapting to various grade levels and social backgrounds of students.

SOME PROMISING SCHOOL PROGRAMS

Some schools and school systems have developed programs aimed at helping poorly educated and low-income parents contribute to their children's schooling. The Parents Plus program in Chicago brings such parents into the school one day a week to learn how they can help at home with current school work and to expand their homemaking and community-related skills. On a less ambitious scale, many schools encourage "make it, take it" sessions where parents can make inexpensive educational aids and learn how to use them at home. Other schools give parents calendars with simple daily home learning activity suggestions or booklets with more general tips.

The Home and School Institute has developed "home learning recipes" that build family interaction and academic progress without duplicating school activities. Easy to follow and aimed at improving basic skills, they have been adopted by various school systems for use in elementary school projects (Rich and others, 1979). The Houston Failsafe program gives parents computer-generated individualized suggestions for improving their children's performance in deficient areas. Large numbers of parents attend the well-publicized conferences with teachers where these suggestions are discussed. The Philadelphia School District pioneered the use of telephone hotlines to help students with homework problems and to inform parents of school events and provide them with educational advice.

Most of these programs were identified in a recent survey of home-school partnership programs in the upper elementary and secondary schools in the 24 largest American cities (Collins and others, 1982). Twenty-eight programs were found that involved parents in improving the school performance and social development of their children. Half were targeted on low-income families, but many were also citywide programs capable of reaching educationally disadvantaged students from all walks of life.

To involve parents, the programs used individual conferences, workshops or classes, and home visits or telephone calls to parents. Most saw achievement in reading and math as a major goal, but half or more were also concerned with attendance or social development. Eighteen of the 28 programs expected parents to tutor their children at home; 21 sought to use parents in broader socializing roles; and 19 helped parents plan their children's home and community educational experiences. In many places parents and educators have overcome the distance, fears, and other barriers that have separated them in the past.

These programs reported some very encouraging results: reduced absenteeism, higher achievement scores, improved student behavior, and restored confidence and participation among parents. Eighteen saw greater parent support and communication with the schools, and 11 reported greater parent participation in their children's learning and development. Whether these gains and changes in behavior can be attributed directly to stronger home-school relationships is difficult to assess, but it would be useful to explore this possibility further.

TEACHER PRACTICES

Individual teachers have also developed a wide range of practices for participating parents. Becker and Epstein (1982) have identified 14 techniques for involving parents in teaching activities at home and examined their use in a statewide survey of 3,700 elementary school teachers. The techniques were subsequently clustered into five approaches:

- Activities emphasizing reading, such as asking parents to read to their children or listen to them read.
- Learning through discussion, such as asking parents to watch a special television program with their children and discuss it afterward.
- Informal learning activites at home, such as sending home ideas for family games or activities related to school work.
- Contracts between teachers and parents, such as formal agreements for parents to supervise and assist children with homework.
- Developing teaching and evaluation skills in parents, such as explaining techniques for teaching or for making learning materials.

The most popular approach involved parents in reading instruction. Its use declined from first to fifth grade, as did use of informal learning activities and development of teaching skills. But the use of contracts, television-stimulated family discussion, parent evaluation forms, and assignments to ask parents questions were used as often with older students as with younger children.

Teachers reported the most contact with parents of children who had learning or discipline problems or parents who were already assisting in the school. Teachers with more black students used more of the five parent involvement techniques even after statistically controlling for student academic and behavioral characteristics, parents' education, and other possible variables. This study did not, however, support the common belief that teachers are best able to work with better educated parents. Education level was unrelated to use of specific techniques. The *belief* that poorly educated parents cannot help seems more a consequence of not having used the methods. According to Becker and Epstein (1982), "When the school conditions are poor, when learning problems are severe, when many students need more help than the teacher has time to give, teachers may be more likely to seek help from parents and to assist parents in workshops to provide the help they need."

Teachers' *attitudes* toward use of parent involvement techniques were not closely related to their actual *use* of the techniques, although most teachers said they needed and wanted parents' assistance. It was interesting that measures of professsional climate in their schools had little effect on teachers' practices and attitudes. Support from the principal was related only to the development of parent training workshops, and the practices of other teachers in the school were unrelated to the practice or opinion of parent involvement. Apparently teachers can develop parent involvement strategies without strong nearby support, though it has many advantages.

CONCLUSIONS

From what we know so far about parent involvement, some themes are beginning to emerge. First, the interest in parent participation is clear, strong, and specific from all sides. Second, while the obstacles are many, educators need to re-examine prevailing beliefs about parents, their capabilities, and interests. It is noteworthy that teachers in one large survey employed a range of parent involvement practices equally as often with poorly educated as with better educated parents (Becker and Epstein, 1982). Also, working mothers help as much with school work and other forms of participation with student learning as do nonemployed mothers, even in the early adolescent years (Medrich, 1982; Tangri and Leitch, 1982).

A third theme is the interest in parent participation beyond the early elementary grades. Where children's basic reading and math skills continue to lag, parents may be able to draw on their own knowledge to help their older children, even if they do not have a high level of education. With high school students, parents in Houston are attracted to parent-teacher conferences because they know they will get test information on their children's occupational interests and the steps necessary to achieve their career goals (Collins and others, 1982).

A fourth theme is the incomplete and evolving nature of research information on parent participation. Different contact techniques may be more appropriate with certain kinds of schools and families, and some kinds of parental assistance may be more easily applied and more beneficial for student learning than others. Sorting out these conditions will take time, the experience of practitioners, and additional study to clarify ambiguous findings to date.

Beyond these themes is the actual development of parent participation programs and practices in schools. Certain strategies seem especially useful (Burns, 1982; Collins and others, 1982). Including teachers and parents in the development of the program can build a sense of shared ownership and a realistic assessment of needs, commitment, and resources on the part of each. Staff training and orientation in relations with culturally different people, conferencing techniques, and other aspects of dealing with parents are at present largely absent. Clear specification and communication of parent and staff roles are needed to make expectations explicit and commonly understood.

Personal contact may be required to recruit parents, who need training if asked for detailed assistance. Special efforts may be required to accommodate diverse circumstances of parents. Evening and weekend meeting times are necessary to reach working mothers and fathers. Recognition of parent contributions can boost their cooperation and sense of involvement. Within the school system, computers can be used to generate more individualized information on students and prescriptions for parent assistance than was previously possible.

These and other techniques and strategies can make home-school relationships function well. Overarching these specifics, and perhaps most important to a successful parent participation program, is the whole-hearted commitment of teachers, schools, and school systems.

REFERENCES

Becker, H. J., and Epstein, J. L. "Influences on Teachers' Use of Parent Involvement at Home." Report No. 324. Baltimore: Johns Hopkins University Center for Social Organization of Schools, 1982.

Benson, C. S.; Buckley, S.; and Medrich, E. A. "Families as Educators: Time Use Contributions to School Achievement." In *School Finance Policy in the 1980's: A Decade of Conflict.* Edited by J. Guthrie. Cambridge, Mass.: Ballinger, 1980.

Bronfenbrenner, Urie. *Is Early Intervention Effective? A Report on Longitudinal Evaluations of Preschool Programs. Volume II.* Washington, D.C.: Department of Health, Education and Welfare, 1974.

Brookover, W. B., and others. *School Social Systems and Student Achievement: Schools Can Make a Difference.* New York: Praeger, 1979.

Burns, J. "The Study of Parental Involvement in Four Federal Education Programs: Executive Summary." Washington, D.C.: Department of Education, Office of Planning, Budget and Evaluation, 1982.

Collins, C. H.; Moles, O. C.; and Cross, M. *The Home-School Connection: Selected Partnership Programs in Large Cities.* Boston: Institute for Responsive Education, 1982.

Gallup, G. H. "The 10th Annual Gallup Poll of the Public's Attitudes Toward the Public Schools." *Phi Delta Kappan* 60 (1978): 33-45.

Henderson, A. *Parent Participation—Student Achievement: The Evidence Grows.* Columbia, Md.: National Committee for Citizens in Education, 1981.

Lightfoot, Sara Lawrence. *Worlds Apart.* New York: Basic Books, 1978.

Medrich, E. A., and others. *The Serious Business of Growing Up: A Study of Children's Lives Outside of School.* Berkeley: University of California Press, 1982.

NEA. "Nationwide Teacher Opinion Poll." Washington, D.C.: National Education Association Research Memo, 1981.

Phi Delta Kappa. *Why Do Some Schools Succeed? The Phi Delta Kappa Study of Exceptional Urban Elementary Schools.* Bloomington, Ind.: Phi Delta Kappa, 1980.

Rich, D.; Mattox, B.; and Van Dien, Jr. "Building on Family Strengths: The 'Nondeficit' Involvement Model for Teaming Home and School." *Educational Leadership* 36 (April 1979): 506-510.

Tangri, S. S., and Leitch, M. L. "Barriers to Home-School Collaboration: Two Case Studies in Junior High Schools." Final report submitted to The National Institute of Education. Washington, D.C.: The Urban Institute, May 1982.

Williams, D. L. "Final Interim Report: Southwest Parent Education Resource Center." Austin, Tex.: Southwest Educational Development Laboratory, 1981.

APPENDIX C. ISSUES AND EMPHASES OF THE PARENT INVOLVEMENT MOVEMENT

A CHILD RESOURCE POLICY: MOVING BEYOND DEPENDENCE ON SCHOOL AND FAMILY*

by Shirley Brice Heath and Milbrey Wallin McLaughlin

Expressions of concern about the competencies and future of the nation's schoolchildren are not new. Americans began to voice doubts about the graduates of their schools shortly after World War II, when the curriculum seemed unable to meet the challenges of global citizenship and when public education began to move away from the rural or small-town model that had characterized it for more than a century.[1]

In the 1950s the concern sharpened when challenges from the Soviet Union brought the U.S. educational system up short. The American response was to blame the schools. New criteria, innovative teaching methods, and tailored technologies entered classrooms to transmit to children the knowledge that educators believed they needed to prepare them for competition with Soviet youth.

In the 1960s and 1970s, when the failure of these changes to bring about the desired improvements in the competitive position of U.S. workers became evident, policy makers blamed the victims and their environments. The disadvantages of blighted urban environments, rural poverty, and cultural and linguistic differences held children back, they said. They suggested that the only redemption for children lay in focusing on the problems of society—fixing up urban centers, reinvigorating rural life, and acknowledging ethnic history while pushing for the timeless economic rewards of sociocultural assimilation. New schemes for school finance and new plans for meeting state needs with categorical funding were developed. "Fixing" societal institutions was supposed to lead to remedies that would improve education for children.

---

*From *Phi Delta Kappan*, April 1987, pp. 576-79. © 1987, Phi Delta Kappan, Inc. Reprinted with permission.

In the 1970s public response to the problems of schooling tended to focus on single issues, such as functional illiteracy, neglect of the basics, and holding teachers accountable. The prevalence of such views of schooling brought with it a series of state and federal actions that seemed to blame the teacher. Statewide testing of teachers' knowledge bases, evaluation schemes to assess in-class performance, and programs of individualized instruction that tied teachers to prescribed and presequenced measures of student performance placed the blame for poor student performance squarely on teachers' shoulders.

In the early 1980s, however, reports that addressed the issue of teacher preparation—notably *A Nation at Risk*—warned that singling out teachers for blame because of the unsatisfactory academic performance of students greatly oversimplified the way learning takes place in contemporary society. This report cautioned that education for the 21st century could not be limited to a single institution and that piecemeal approaches to reform that ignored the interdependent nature of the workplace, families, schools, and community institutions were doomed from the start.

In the mid-1980s, at least partly in response to the acknowledged complexity of learning in today's society, another component of "the problem" of inadequately prepared young people was brought to the fore: parents. Deficiencies in parenting and in families, this new analysis runs, lie at the core of students' identified inadequacies as future workers, citizens, and parents. Thus many policy makers and school districts are trying to involve parents as partners in the education of their children.

In contrast to the politically based, formalized parent participation models of the preceding era (1965–1980), which failed to elicit widespread or long-term parent involvement, today's strategies stress parents as extensions of the schools' business—supporters of homework, monitors of activities, and reinforcers of school values.[2] Policy makers hope that cooperative efforts between parents and schools will help increase in-home support for educational goals and activities, as well as make school personnel more sensitive to realities of the family. They hope that, by working together, parents and schools can provide the ingredients for school success, academic achievement, and so a productive future for American youth.

This latest assault on the "education problem" will, we fear, be no more successful in equipping the nation's children for the future than were those that came before. To be sure, the rationale for turning to parents is clear. The inability or unwillingness of American families to socialize, support, stimulate, and encourage their children in the ways and objectives of the schools lies at the root of the disappointing educational attainments cited by blue-ribbon commissions, special panels, and public officials.

However compelling the analysis of the roles of parents and families in their children's educational experience, the expectation that bringing family and school together will set children on their way to productive adulthood ignores current societal realities and is, we believe, mistaken. Such strategies are critically limited for two reasons.

First, they take a narrow view of the "outcomes" of schooling as academic achievement. Although academic achievement has traditionally been the express purpose of the schools and has been taken as sufficient proof of their success, academic achievement alone does not guarantee the effective citizens and adults America requires. Other outcomes must be accomplished concurrently in order for academic achievement to mean much. These nonacademic outcomes build on notions of social competence and include additional dimensions, such as physical and mental health, formal cognition, and motivational and emotional status.[3] This broader view of outcomes raises questions about the extent to which these complementary and necessary functions can be served by today's schools or families, acting singly or in concert. In this sense, then, we believe today's education reform initiatives are inadequate.

But the issue is more than a narrow conception of outcome. The second reason that these home/school partnership policies are limited stems from the unreviewed and outdated assumptions about the role of families and the role of schools on which they are built. Today's schools build on yesterday's notion of "family," both in form and function. Schools as social institutions have become outmoded, because the institutions on which they depend—particularly the family and the workplace—have changed dramatically. Demographic, economic, and cultural changes (especially since World War II) have shifted patterns of family alignment, mobility, workplace/family relations, ethnic and linguistic composition, and age structure of the population; these changes have altered the very definition of "family" and the role that even the idealized, nuclear family can play in the education of children today.

For example, in 1986 only 7% of families could be described as the "typical" family that shaped the Great Society legislation of the mid-1960s: a two-parent family in which working fathers and homemaking mothers provided sustenance, structure, and support for school-age children. Many families, including privileged ones, can provide only uneven support for their children's school experience. Real or perceived economic pressures weigh on most households. Most parents feel compelled to work long hours—or more than one job—simply to keep family finances on track or to provide the standard of living that Americans have come to expect. Dual-career families, like single-parent families, have precious little time or energy to spend working as partners in their children's education, visiting the school, attending conferences, or providing extracurricular activities for their children. The extended family, previously shown to provide essential support to stressed nuclear families and to distinguish the children from such troubled families who nonetheless became competent adults,[4] is practically extinct.

And even the basic maintenance functions of families, assumed by traditional models of public education, often go unmet. For example, even in advantaged suburbs, teachers report that some children come to school insufficiently socialized in the manners and expectations of public education. In poorer neighborhoods, children arrive each morning lacking as well such fundamental necessities as breakfast, supplies, and clean clothing. Families may be "here to stay,"[5] but they have changed radically in structure and function in the past three decades and bear scant resemblance to the family for which contemporary school policy is modeled.

Other changes in American families have equally important—but often less obvious—consequences for the role of the school and its ability to prepare children for the future. In particular, cultural and linguistic factors undermine traditional assumptions of family/school interactions. The high percentage (projected to exceed 50% by the year 2000) of the nation's school-age children who represent ethnolinguistic and cultural minorities bring substantively different resources to school than do children from the cultural mainstream. These children bring different amounts and types of "cultural capital" to apply to the task of schooling.

For example, within those families strongly oriented toward schooling, community institutions, and commercial socialization services (such as ballet classes, tennis and piano lessons, and summer camps), children learn numerous ways to use language. They have extensive experience in learning by listening to others tell how to do something, they themselves know how to talk about what they are doing as they do it, and they know how to lay out plans for the future in verbal form. On command, they know how to display in oral or written formats the bits and pieces of knowledge that the school assumes represent academic achievement.

Children from families whose traditional orientations to learning have been observing and assuming apprenticeship roles beside knowledgeable elders come to school largely untutored in displaying knowledge in verbal form.[6] Parents who do not speak English, keen to have their children learn English rapidly, often stop speaking their mother tongue to their children. This not only denies children the necessary exposure to adult language models, but also denies them access to the wisdom and authority of their parents.

Cultural capital differs among families in more than linguistic style or facility. Children also come to school with different perceptions of and exposure to the multiple resources that support education. For example, in homes in which English is not the first language, the relative infrequency of written guides to action stands in sharp contrast to the pervasive use in mainstream homes of newspapers, magazines, and how-to books that serve as guides to movie selection, vacation and financial planning, menu planning, the remodeling of kitchens, or gardening.

More recently arrived language minority groups (such as the Vietnamese) who entered the United States under church sponsorship and with support from local community organizations have fared much better in schools and employment than those groups (such as migrants of Mexican origin) who have had to rely primarily on family networks.[7] The family and school have not been able to give the latter the linguistic and cultural capital they need in contemporary society. When schools attempt to involve parents from these families—many of which are either single-parent or have both parents working—in the education of their children, the parents feel inadequate and insecure. They often acquiesce to the authority of the school—erroneously believing that by listening, remaining quiet, and obeying, their children will achieve school success and preparation for better jobs than the low-skilled service jobs the parents perform.[8]

These cultural, demographic, and economic realities have fundamentally altered the functions families play and the possible shapes parent/school partnerships can take. Family- or parent-centered policies are no more likely to "fix" the problems of American youth and the public schools than were the other single-issue, school-based policies that preceded them. These family-focused remedies are unlikely to succeed, because they ignore the structural realities of today's families, the resources available to them, and their ability to interact with the school.

One consequence of the changed role of the family as a social institution is the undermining of traditional institutional conceptions of the school. Out-of-school functions that are essential to productive adulthood or social competence often go unfulfilled for many children. Thus refurbished curricula, better teachers, and productive parent/school partnerships are bound to fall short of achieving the nation's goals for its youth.

The debate need not end with this pessimistic assessment of the limits of present conceptions of school and family. However, the foregoing analysis suggests that a broader view of the strategies and institutions necessary to social competence is required. For example, those children who succeed academically and emotionally in today's world and move on to adulthood with a sense of dignity and self-worth have typically depended on more than families and schools.[9] Academically successful children from non-mainstream backgrounds are children who have widened their net of social participation beyond the home and schoolyard to encompass such community offerings as work experience, athletics, Scouting, and any of a host of others.

For families in which both parents work, for single-parent families, and even for seemingly storybook-perfect nuclear families, community institutions and volunteer agencies can give their children access to adults with a wide range of talents and perspectives not likely to be found within a single family. These institutions can place children in the dual roles of workers and learners, of group members and individual performers. These out-of-school educational activities provide opportunities for experiential learning that not only motivates students to pursue academic learning, but also orients them to the constant need to readjust—to respond to changes in institutional leadership and to unexpected pressures from the larger society. (Consider, for example, the civic lessons learned by youngsters in city recreational programs beset by current liability insurance woes.) Supplementing the contributions of school and family in silent and unacknowledged ways, these community institutions promote youngsters' curiosity about the causes of new policies and practices and offer a sense of the interdependence of societal institutions.

Community organizations and out-of-school opportunities for work and play have grown quietly as appendages of the school and family, affirming and supporting the efforts of educators and parents. Family demographics, the demands of the contemporary professional workplace, the wage structure that requires two-wage-earner households, and the multiplicity of sociocultural groups have made community organizations necessary and allowed them to persist, despite severely reduced funding. Big Brothers and Big Sisters, community libraries, after-school tutoring fellowships, and children's drama workshops—all of which are supported by donations and operate on shoestring budgets—demonstrate that traditional models of family/school relations no longer reflect reality.

The problems of family/school relations in the 1980s have multiple causes that are too complex, too varied, too enmeshed with larger social realities to respond to single-policy solutions, such as parent partnerships, parent involvement mechanisms, and the like. Daniel Patrick Moynihan has said that "family deterioration neither proceeds from nor responds to efforts at relief."[10] The same is true of deterioration in family/school relations since the early 1940s.[11]

The assumptions that underlie these solutions are fundamentally misaligned with today's social realities. All the policy responses to the problems of education and to the perceived deficiencies in the public schools—more testing, greater accountability, tougher graduation requirements, new curricula, changed financing strategies, required participation of parents—share a common feature. They are instrumental responses that focus on strategic aspects of the education "delivery system" and attempt to standardize the component parts to achieve a more effective education for all children. But none begins with a consideration of the *functions* of educating, nurturing, and supporting that are required to develop competent adults in light of the institutional resources available. Yet tinkering—adding a little of this and a little of that to contemporary families and schools—has proved inadequate to the task.

The problems of educational achievement and academic success demand resources beyond the scope of the schools and of most families. We believe that promising responses can be crafted by moving from a focus on components of the problem—teachers, texts, families—to a focus on the functional requirements of a healthy, curious, productive, and motivated child. This change in perspective draws attention to the child as an actor in a larger social system and to the institutional networks and resources present in that larger environment. It requires us to look beyond family and school to get a full view of the primary networks that make up a child's environment. We can then think of the school in a new way, as a nexus of institutions within this environment.

In this view, the school moves from the role of "deliverer" of educational services to the role of "broker" of the multiple services that can be used to achieve the functions previously filled by families or by families and schools acting together.[12] Some schools and communities have already begun such efforts. Alonzo Crim, superintendent of the Atlanta Public Schools, has enlisted community resources and individual mentors for schoolchildren; dramatic improvements in standardized test scores and in school attendance have resulted. In New Haven, Connecticut, the Yale Child Welfare Research Program has demonstrated both the possibility and the promise of integrating and focusing multiple community-based resources on young children.[13]

The Bread Loaf School of English at Middlebury College in Vermont has brought rural teachers of English from across the nation to Middlebury where they learn to correspond with farm service agency personnel, programs for dropout mothers, and adult literacy groups. These teachers then convey the same skills to their students, who no longer see their school tasks of reading, writing, and intepreting texts as set off from the daily challenges of economic and social survival in economically depressed rural America.

In urban areas, a few business groups are cooperating with mathematics and English teachers to offer workers and students a chance to get together to examine the ways in which school knowledge relates to job success. Several major universities now offer undergraduates a variety of public service opportunities that do more than feed students' temporary urges to "do good." Students in these programs keep records of their activities. Then, in group seminars, they reflect on relations between such voluntary efforts and the structures of business organizations.

These diverse examples have a number of common features that inform a changed conception of the school and its role in society. Each builds on local resources, meets local needs, and makes use of local conceptions of ways to keep the generally static skills and knowledge imparted by the school and the family attuned to the changing demands of business and the community. Each is broadly based and recognizes the dynamic nature of community resources. Each strategy is multiplex, moving from isolated action to interdependent initiative. Each moves from the disciplinary, professional, political, and bureaucratic isolation that characterized education and social policies of the past to an integrated view of children as members of a larger social system. And, perhaps most critically, each is rooted in a functional analysis of transitional objectives for children, rather than aimed solely at the transmission of skills and knowledge.

The focus of these new strategies is on preparing children as learners for the varying types of learning they must accomplish as they take up a variety of roles throughout their development. The focus is no longer on assessing deficiencies in the components of the educational delivery system—parents, teachers, curriculum, schools—but on identifying and coordinating the social networks of children.

The societal responsibility for educating children necessitates a changed governance structure and planning across the traditional boundaries of the public and private sectors. The school becomes the nexus for community, business, and family collaboration that places academic learning within the nurturant ecosystem of athletic, vocational and service-oriented agencies and institutions dedicated to mental and physical health. No longer would school boards and district offices focus on the school as a separate institution and attempt to meet only parental demands. Instead, district and state personnel would bring together representatives of local community agencies, businesses, and athletic groups to decide on shared goals and general strategies for providing coordinated partnership efforts to meet these goals.

Some might argue that there is little about which all these groups would agree. To the contrary, we believe that there is *much* on which all would agree. Different though their activities may be, these institutions share a common concern for the productive development of children. For example, coaches of Little League baseball, English teachers, employers, and public health workers all teach respect for carrying out certain tasks within specified blocks of time and require young people to translate written information into oral restatements and direct follow-up action. All these agencies—recreational, academic, vocational, and health—operate by involving their adult members in group decision making and cooperative task fulfillment. And all expect their individual members to be able to speak as representatives of these groups.

Each institution has a unique and necessary contribution to make to the development of academically successful, motivated, healthy, and effective children. Their combined contributions form the heart of a child resource policy and combine to create a network of reciprocal functions that can succeed where single-focus reforms have failed.

Yet the vision of such a social network makes tough demands on policy makers, practitioners, and planners. It requires coordination and collaboration among bureaucracies and professional groups that have entrenched notions of "turf" and entitlements. It also requires moving from the time-honored (and sometimes serviceable) strategy of making incremental policy adjustments in existing institutions to a radically different conception of the school and its role in preparing the nation's youth for tomorrow's workplace, family, and community.

FOOTNOTES

[1] James P. Comer, "Home-School Relationships as They Affect the Academic Success of Children," *Education and Urban Society*, vol. 16, 1984, pp. 323-37.

[2] Henry Jay Becker and Joyce Epstein, "Parent Involvement: A Survey of Teacher Practices," *Elementary School Journal*, vol. 83, 1982, pp. 277-94; and Dorothy Rich, "Helping Parents Help Their Children Learn," *Educational Leadership*, April 1985, p. 80.

[3] Edward Zigler and Penelope Trickett, "I.Q., Social Competence, and Evaluation of Early Childhood Intervention Programs," *American Psychologist*, vol. 33, 1978, pp. 789-98.

[4] Emmy Werner and Ruth Smith, *Vulnerable but Invincible: A Longitudinal Study of Resilient Children and Youth* (New York: McGraw-Hill, 1982).

[5] Mary Jo Bane, *Here to Stay* (New York: Basic Books, 1976).

[6] Shirley Brice Heath, *Ways with Words: Language, Life, and Work in Communities and Classrooms* (Cambridge: Cambridge University Press, 1983).

[7] California State Department of Education, *Beyond Language: Social and Cultural Factors in Schooling Language Minority Students* (Sacramento, Calif.: Bilingual Education Office, 1985).

[8] Stephen H. Wilson, "Strengthening Connections Between Schools and Communities: A Method of Improving Urban Schools," *Urban Education*, July 1983, pp. 153-77.

[9] Eldon E. Snyder and Elmer Spreitzer, *Social Aspects of Sport*, 2nd ed. (Englewood Cliffs, N.J.: Prentice-Hall, 1983).

[10] Daniel Patrick Moynihan, *Family and Nation* (New York: Harcourt Brace Jovanovich, 1986), p. 158.

[11] Comer, "Home-School Relationships. . . ."

[12] Nicholas Hobbs, "Families, Schools, and Communities: An Ecosystem for Children," *Teachers College Record*, vol. 79, 1978, pp. 756-66; Edward Zigler and Heather Weiss, "Family Support Systems: An Ecological Approach to Child Development," in Robert N. Rapoport, ed., *Children, Youth, and Families: The Action-Research Relationship* (Cambridge: Cambridge University Press, 1985), pp. 166-205; Wilson, "Strengthening Connections. . ."; and Elsie Smith and Clement B. G. London, "A Union of School, Community, and Family," *Urban Education*, vol. 16, 1981, pp. 247-60.

[13] Zigler and Weiss, "Family Support. . . ."

LET'S NOT THROW OUT THE BABY WITH THE BATH WATER*

by Dorothy Rich

I have agreed with so much that Milbrey McLaughlin has written that I find it surprising that the article by her and Shirley Brice Heath in the April 1987 issue of the *Kappan*, "A Child Resource Policy: Moving Beyond Dependence on School and Family," contains assumptions and statements of fact that are not only questionable but wrong. I do not disagree with all that Heath and McLaughlin say in the article, but, in the comments that follow, I cite those parts of the article with which I do disagree and indicate in what ways I believe they are misleading, unclear, inexplicable, or in need of additional information.

Quote: Many of today's strategies for school renewal emphasize parental involvement in the work of the school. This emphasis is misplaced and rests on outdated assumptions. . . .

Fact: In June 1986 McLaughlin wrote the following in her paper, "Involving Parents in Schools: Lessons for Policy" (co-author, Patrick Shields): "Should parent involvement be a policy priority? Even if it 'works,' should parent involvement concern policy makers, given the multiple, competing demands for policy attention? We believe the answer is 'yes.' Parent involvement merits significant policy attention and public resources primarily for two reasons. One stems from strong evidence that low-income and poorly educated parents *want* to help and want to play a role in their child's education. . . . What's lacking, in most schools and districts, are strategies or structures appropriate to the involvement of these parents."[1]

What's happened in the last year? To my knowledge, no studies or experiences have occurred that would abrogate McLaughlin's statement of June 1986. It is inexplicable why only one year later her point of view has changed so markedly.

---

*From *Phi Delta Kappan*, June 1987, pp. 784-85. © 1987, Phi Delta Kappan, Inc. Reprinted with permission.

Why is it that no sooner do we try to launch something in education than we say it doesn't work? That's like taking half a dose of penicillin and saying that it just won't do the job.

Quote: Thus many policy makers and school districts are trying to involve parents as partners in the education of their children.

Fact: How I wish this were true! But the facts are different. While rhetoric about the family's role in education continues to grow, efforts to put this rhetoric into action are only modest and fragmentary. There is a definite parent gap in the education reform movement. For example, I could not find the word *family* mentioned in the much-heralded Carnegie Report. Reform activities and initiatives include such traditional topics as career ladders, competency tests for teachers, higher graduation requirements, and limitations on extracurricular activities for students. No state, to my knowledge, has identified family/school involvement as a key strategy to be used to address education issues.

Quote: Today's schools build on yesterday's notion of "family," both in form and function. . . . For example, only 7% of families could be described as the "typical" family that shaped the Great Society legislation of the mid-1960s. . . .

Fact: For years, we've been told that there is no longer any family out there. But this is just not true. Statistics and experience tell us otherwise. First the statistics: 70% of our population continue to live in married-couple households.[2]

Figures showing very low numbers for traditional families, such as the 7% quoted by Heath and McLaughlin, are alarmist. This implies that the family has collapsed altogether. Such statements assume a specific family of a certain size, such as two children. Married-couple households with exactly two children under 18 in which the mother never was employed have never constituted the overwhelming majority of families in this country.

In fact, 74% of our children now live in two-parent households and, while women are employed in vastly greater numbers, even today 33% of our children have mothers who are not in the labor force at all. Another 37% of our children have mothers who work only part-time or part-year. Twenty-seven percent of all children under 18 have a mother who works full-time, year round.[3]

In short, the family is not dead. My own experience in working with thousands of parents across the nation, many of whom hold more than one job, is that they continue to be caring and concerned parents and that they are eager to strengthen their children's education.

Quote: Many families, including privileged ones, can provide only uneven support for their children's school experience.

Response: Does this mean that we let those families off the hook, that we say that they have no responsibility for the children they have brought into this world? I hope not. Let's not throw out the baby with the bath water. I believe that all families—rich or poor—have the responsibility to provide their children with the values and attitudes that support their children's education.

Quote: The problems of family/school relationships in the 1980s have multiple causes that are too complex, too varied, too enmeshed with larger social realities to respond to single-policy solutions, such as parent partnerships, parent involvement mechanisms, and the like.

Response: Real parent partnerships are not single solutions. I am not talking about setting up advisory councils of parents or even about encouraging volunteers to help out in the classroom, laudable though these kinds of activities may be. I believe that today's parent partnerships must go well past classroom involvement. They must reflect the needs of today's students: to gain skills and attitudes that encompass academics but also extend to the values that will enable children to continue learning after school is over.

This means helping families teach children what I call Mega-Skills®. I call these "our children's inner engines for learning." These are the big values, such as confidence, responsibility, and perseverance that enable children to be "the effective citizens that America requires." I believe this learning is generated at home.

Quote: For families in which both parents work, for single-parent families, and even for seemingly storybook-perfect nuclear families, community institutions and volunteer agencies can give their children access to adults with a wide range of talents and perspectives not likely to be found within a single family.

Reponse: Fine. But bringing this about demands an infrastructure, a set of bridges that I believe must be built on the primary bridge between the school and the family. To date, this primary bridge has not been built. To assume that it has, as Heath and McLaughlin do, is to give me and my pioneering colleagues in the parent-involvement movement credit for more success that we have achieved.

I have been saying for years that schooling must form collaborative arrangements with other agencies in the community. To help do this, the Home and School Institute, with support from the MacArthur Foundation, has just launched New Partnerships for Student Achievement, a project that will work with five major national membership organizations: the American Red Cross, the American Postal Workers Union, the Association for Library Service to Children/American Library Association, the National Association of Colored Women's Clubs, and Parents Without Partners. We are providing family-as-educator programs, so that these organizations can serve their own members and the schools and communities in which they live. Today it is true that not even the best schools can do the job alone. And it's also probably true that not even the best family can do the job alone. We all need one another, but we must find ways to link hands. The new Chapter 1 House Bill includes family-as-educator initiatives for the first time. And Sen. Bill Bradley (D-N.J.) has introduced the new Family-School Partnership Act in the Senate.

Quote: In this view, the school moves from the role of "deliverer" of educational services to the role of "broker" of the multiple services that can be used to achieve the functions previously filled by families or by families and schools acting together.

Response: I agree. In *The Forgotten Factor in School Success— The Family*,[4] I call for training to enable teachers to play this enhanced role to facilitate learning within and outside of the school walls. Indeed, it will take training not just to broker this learning but to help teachers work effectively with adults. When teachers can shift easily from talking to kids to talking *with* adults, then I will feel more confident of the schools' ability to serve as brokers of knowledge among adults.

Finally, Heath and McLaughlin call for a "nurturant ecosystem." It sounds great, but who will be responsible for putting this ecosystem in place and making sure that it continues to function? Perhaps we need "education" boards instead of school boards.

I need to know specifically who will be responsible. When we're told that we're all responsible, then no one is. Perhaps this diffused responsibility would work in California, which is a special state. But I for one want to know whom to call when the ecosystem breaks down.

FOOTNOTES

[1] Milbrey W. McLaughlin and Patrick M. Shields, "Involving Parents in the Schools: Lessons for Policy," paper prepared for the Conference on Effects of Alternative Designs in Compensatory Education, Washington, D.C.: 17–18 June 1986.

[2] U.S. Census Bureau, *Statistical Abstract of the United States* (Washington, D.C.: U.S. Bureau of Labor Statistics, March 1987), p. 45.

[3] House Select Committee on Children, Youth and Family, *U.S. Children and Their Families: Current Conditions and Future Trends* (Washington, D.C.: U.S. Government Printing Office, March 1987).

[4] Dorothy Rich, *The Forgotten Factor in School Success—The Family* (Washington, D.C.: Home and School Institute, 1985), pp. 38–39.

A MATTER OF INTERPRETATION*

by Shirley Brice Heath and Milbrey Wallin McLaughlin

In her critique of our article, Dorothy Rich provides us with a welcome opportunity to reiterate our belief in the importance of strong, vital parent involvement in education and to restate our concerns. We never suggested throwing the baby out with the bath water, as Rich puts it. Instead, we acknowledge the compelling rationale for involving parents in their children's education *as well as* the limits of such a strategy—limits imposed by changing family structures, changing economic realities, and changing demographics.

We believe that the value of parent involvement is not in question. The issue is whether parent involvement strategies, any more than other single-focus policies—better teachers, new texts, or higher standards—can "solve" the grave problems society faces in preparing young people for a productive future.

We agree that present efforts to involve parents are "modest and fragmentary." We also agree that they should be strengthened and expanded. However, we do not agree with those who present parent involvement as a panacea for today's educational ills, nor do we agree with Rich's assessment that parent involvement is largely absent from current reform efforts.

For example, parent involvement is currently a topic of much interest in Congress and in the thinking of key staff members at the Education Department. And, contrary to Rich, we hear parent involvement discussed in many states (California, New York, Florida, South Carolina, Texas, and Arkansas come immediately to mind). Moreover, many of the most popular involvement strategies (e.g., increased involvement in school decision making, active roles for parents in homework and monitoring, parents-as-experts in social studies classes) are largely middle-class models that cannot garner significant participation from disadvantaged, low-income, or non-English-speaking families. Indeed, Rich's own work builds

---

*From *Phi Delta Kappan*, June 1987, p. 786. © 1987, Phi Delta Kappan, Inc. Reprinted with permission.

on this recognition and asserts that poor families need different avenues of involvement.

We do not claim that there is "no family out there," as Rich suggests. Instead, we claim that the family that sends its children to school today (and that will do so tomorrow) is substantially changed from the family that provides the model for yesterday's assumptions about home/school relations. On this point, Rich's own statistics can be read in a number of ways. Perhaps 70% of our population does live in married-couple households. But how many such households have school-age children? And how many have adults who are accessible to the children immediately before and after school? Consider the fact that 44% of today's workforce is female. By 1995 more than 80% of women in their childbearing years are expected to be working.

Other statistics are not alarmist but alarming. Consider that in 1985 nearly one-third of all women between the ages of 35 and 39 who were ever married had already ended a first marriage in divorce; that the parents of at least 40% of children born this year will divorce; and that last year 20.2% of white births and 74.5% of black births were out of wedlock.

And changing family patterns cross class lines. Although parents have an essential role to play in their children's school experience, today's family is severely limited in the definition that role can take. This is true for middle-class families pursuing dual careers and especially true for those families that also battle poverty, violence, and ill health.

In this context, our response to the complex needs of today's children—the child resource policy we called for in our April *Kappan* article—seems entirely consistent with Rich's New Partnerships for Student Achievement. We applaud this new venture, which integrates parents with other community-based resources for children, and we conclude that any disagreement between Dorothy Rich and us has more to do with interpretation than with intent.

APPENDIX D. OPINION

THE COMMUNITY GAP IN EDUCATION REFORM*

by Dorothy Rich

The trouble with education today is not the usual complaint that teachers and parents don't care anymore. The trouble is that there is too much focus on the school. If that sounds like heresy, it is heresy based on educational research and common sense.

The success of schooling ultimately depends on student interest and motivation. Unlike educational reforms that provide for more school buildings or higher teacher salaries, student motivation comes basically from the family.

For over 20 years, I have studied family and community impact on schooling. What I have found is that there is a great deal of rhetoric about parent involvement in schooling. Everyone says it is important, but there is next to no real support for it in practice. There is no real funding for it; there is no teacher training for it; there is no legislative or policy commitment to it.

THE PARENT GAP

The startling parent gap in the educational reform movement is illustrated in the report of the National Commission on Excellence in Education which centers almost exclusively on the school. It addresses parents only in a postscript: "As surely as you are your children's most important teachers, your children's ideas about education and its significance begin with you. Moreover, you bear a responsibility to participate actively in your children's education." These are good words. But words are not enough!

Our Institute experience in national programs with thousands of families indicates that families—even those considered "hard to

---

*From *PEForum*, April 1986. Copyright © 1986 by the Public Education Fund. Reprinted with permission.

reach"—continue to care deeply about their children's education, but they often need help to make the most of the time and the resources they have.

There has been disagreement about what parent involvement is. Some say it is the advisory council at school; some refer to volunteers in the classroom; others talk about "home schooling"—keeping children out of school altogether. In view of today's time constraints, I advocate the kind of parent involvement that is more educationally, personally significant and more equitable for today's family with mothers employed—that is, the involvement of adults with children in learning activities at home, which reinforce and support but do not duplicate the work of the school. My position is that there are strengths in every family that can be mobilized into effective educational action. This involvement, supported by research and confirmed by experience but ignored thus far in educational reforms, provides teaching strategies for families to use at home.

Parent involvement with the most payoffs in test schools and in student motivation is the mobilization of the school and the community's businesses to deliver support to families in their important role in the education of their children. One tested way to do this is described below.

HOME: A SPECIAL LEARNING PLACE

It seems so simple. Maybe it seems too simple. Yet, it is carefully designed and markedly effective. Once a week, in hundreds of schools, what we call home learning "recipes" go home with students. These recipes may call for using the TV schedule to learn to keep to time limits or using newspaper ads to make the best buys at the grocery store. The recipes use things like clocks and cups, and places like supermarkets and gas stations. When you tell parents that with no cost and little time they can teach beginning reading by sorting the laundry or give their child a start on fractions by folding napkins, you provide parents with some of the finest teaching tools found in every home. These recipes are designed to teach reading, writing, and math in un-school-like ways. They do what even the finest schools cannot do. They put the parent and child together for a few minutes each day to learn from one another and to talk together.

In the Teacher-Parent Partnership Project, designed by Home and School Institute for the National Education Association, 6,000 families used these recipes in 1985 with more schools being added this year. Families received them from 140 schools in 10 states, in communities as disparate as Fairbanks, Alaska, to Greenville, South Carolina. But the families were remarkably similar in their responses:

> 91% said that the activities were voluntarily used in their homes; 99% said that the activities helped them spend enjoyable time with their children; 98% said they felt their child learned something useful in doing the activities.

These parents were more than ready to get involved. They did not have to leave their home to go to meetings; they made their contribution to education in their own kitchens and living rooms.

WHAT CAN BE DONE NOW?

What every community needs right now is a campaign to encourage greater awareness of the total community's role (especially families) in the education of children. This campaign has four primary purposes: to involve the media in increasing public understanding of the family's critically important role in children's education; to give parents (and other adults caring for children) practical suggestions for what they can do to help children learn; to involve business as a distributor of parenting and education information to their employees and to their customers; and to ensure that senior citizens and other populations beyond parents are integrated into this community education process.

There is still the prevailing idea that somehow working with families is too complex a task: If only we could tune the school, that seemingly controlled environment, to a finer degree, schooling problems would be solved. While I have great respect for the school (and I am a longtime school teacher), it is clear from our own Institute research and from the research of others that it is like expecting a three-legged stool to stand firmly on one leg, that of the school alone.

The discouragement about the family today is unfounded. Yes,

I know the statistics, but more importantly, I know what happens when you reach out to work with families. They care, and they want to help their children. Across the states, we have successfully reached thousands of what have been called "hard to reach" families. These families, who may not go to meetings in schools because they are employed or otherwise school-avoidant, given encouragement and ideas on how to get involved directly with their child at home, prove to be dedicated and remarkably able home-style teachers for their children. They are giving the message to their children that learning is important.

Teachers are recognizing more than ever the need to work in partnership with parents and with the community; many need training to do this effectively. The public may have to hear that it is a sign of strength, not of weakness, for schools to reach out for help. And, importantly, there is today a strong interest in self-help. To meet this demand and to provide a practical way for business to reach families beyond more traditional school/business partnerships, we are now developing a new parenting program for business entitled "Careers and Caring." These are home and job learning recipes that employers provide to their employees and to customers. This program is designed to support the work of the schools by addressing daily life family concerns.

In the brief space here, there is no way to present all of our training programs and materials and the ways you can use them. But believe me, I am not offering blue-sky theory. Everything I have mentioned has worked where it has been tried. It can be used in many more places.

This is a special time of bipartisan concern and of opportunity. When families see themselves as educators, it takes nothing away from the schools. What is needed is a complementary, nonadversarial partnership that mobilizes the strengths of the home, the school, and the community.

APPENDIX E. RECOMMENDATIONS FOR POLICYMAKERS

PARENT INVOLVEMENT IN EDUCATION: WHAT CAN POLICYMAKERS DO?*

by Dorothy Rich and James Van Dien

The problems facing American education are not problems of the school alone. To be resolved successfully, they must address the relationship of the home, the community, and the school. In testimony in 1986 before the National Governors Association (NGA) Task Force on Parent Involvement and Choice, the president of the Home and School Institute (HSI) outlined the critical "parent gap" in the education reform movement.

This *Issue Paper* offers five specific steps for policymakers that elaborate upon the NGA testimony—steps that can be taken now across the country to provide solutions to the "parent gap" problem by supporting the educational role of the family. Based on demonstrated research, it lays out practical, low-cost methods to enhance the impact of schooling by involving the family.

The chart that follows is specially designed to identify the follow-through, complementary actions that need to be taken at the state and local level. To carry out these recommendations, policymakers will choose from a variety of methods appropriate for their state.

---

*Copyright © 1986 by the Home and School Institute.

OBJECTIVE	STATE LEADERSHIP AND ENABLING ROLE	ACTION NEEDED AT THE LOCAL LEVEL
1. WIDE-SCALE INVOLVEMENT OF FAMILIES IN THE EDUCATION OF THEIR CHILDREN To build on the significant research supporting the family role as educator, over other more traditional parent involvement roles such as volunteers in school and advisory councils. To promote equity in parent involvement focusing on what *all* parents can do *at home*, rather than at school, which limits the number of parents who can participate.	Form a statewide Task Force on Families as Educators to: Set into motion a media information campaign on the importance of the family in education. Provide support for PSA radio and TV spots and newspaper ads on what the family can do at home. Obtain home learning systems, such as those developed by HSI, to provide to localities to distribute to families and schools. Direct state teacher training institutions and in-service programs in school systems to provide training for teachers on how to involve parents in helping their own children. Ask or require that state funded programs such as Principals' Academies provide training to administrators on how to prepare teachers for work with families.	Assemble local task forces of educators, parents, and business people to generate and carry out plans for distribution of home learning activities at all places serving families: schools, clinics, businesses, etc. Establish Family Resource Centers at schools and businesses, perhaps staffed by senior citizens, where parents can meet to get information and materials on child rearing and education. Allocate resources to ensure that educators receive training and materials for work with families. Use school functions to promote the message and practice of family involvement in children's learning. Actions above can be carried out by local authorities such as the school board and the mayor's office.

OBJECTIVE	STATE LEADERSHIP AND ENABLING ROLE	ACTION NEEDED AT THE LOCAL LEVEL
2. FAMILY SELF-HELP FOR PREVENTION OF CHILDREN'S LEARNING AND GROWING-UP DIFFICULTIES To ensure that families know what to do before children come to school. To provide for continuing family support as children progress to adolescence.	Formulate regulations and/or funding support for training preschool child care providers to enhance the academic development of children before they get to school. Use cable television access wherever possible to reach people where they live. Ask or require school systems and schools of education to provide training to junior high teachers on how parents can continue to help their maturing youngsters.	Distribute information and/or provide training to parents when they are still in the hospital with their baby. Provide continuing follow-up materials for parents at doctors' offices and well-baby clinics. Encourage teachers to form parent-to-parent peer support groups. Actions above can be taken by hospitals, social service agencies, and schools.
3. CONNECTING YOUNG AND OLD To take advantage of the untapped resource in education for helping families and schools—the growing number of vigorous senior citizens in our society today.	Establish a statewide Intergenerational Council, composed of representatives of young and old, educators, community leaders, business, and media. This council will provide leadership and formulate strategies for developing programs at the local level involving teachers, seniors, and families. Encourage the use of already developed programs such as HSI's Senior Corps curricula, which involve seniors in teaching basic skills in the classroom and in connecting with families.	Set up local Intergenerational Councils, patterned after the state model. This council will provide leadership for local young/old events. Contact senior centers and schools to bring seniors and teachers and families together. Focus on the role of the senior as friend to the family and as tutor to the youngster. Actions above can be taken by local authorities, such as the mayor's office, to form the council.

OBJECTIVE	STATE LEADERSHIP AND ENABLING ROLE	ACTION NEEDED AT THE LOCAL LEVEL
4. PROVIDING AN INTEGRAL ROLE FOR BUSINESS IN EDUCATION REFORM To add the family dimension to the school/business partnership. To enable business to express its caring for the families of its employees and customers.	Establish or expand the scope of a statewide School/Business Roundtable or Advisory Council: add representative family membership and ask council to focus on ways that it can support the work of the family in educating children. Provide an information kit to local communities on how businesses can get involved with schools and families. Consider use of materials such as HSI's parenting information service for business, *Careers and Caring*. Provide for ways, such as a governor's flag or commendation, that the state can use to honor businesses that reach out to families.	Provide information, especially home learning activities, to customers and to employees. Use materials provided by state council; duplicate in quantity, with own business logo. Set aside sections of stores or factories as places for parents to pick up information—family resource materials—before and after work. Support local media ads carrying the message that families are educators. Actions above can be taken by local business.
5. ENSURING CONTINUATION AND EXPANSION OF FAMILY INVOLVEMENT EFFORTS To establish an infrastructure for coordinating and building upon initial family involvement activities.	Establish an Office of Family Involvement with the governor's office and/or the Department of Education. This office will function across all grade levels and connect with all school subjects. The state office disseminates information and encourages the adoption and replication of model programs developed from across the nation or within the state.	Set up an Office for Family Involvement in the school system to support home-school liaison work at every school. Train paraprofessionals for the specific job of working to connect home and school. Action can be taken by local authority (mayor's office or school board) liaison office to coordinate family involvement activities in the community.

CURRENT MOMENTUM AND OPPORTUNITIES

School and family responsibilities are increasing and will increase even more in the near future. Before 1990, there will be more young children in school and more mothers in the workplace. For more students to succeed, it is vital to enable families to have greater positive impact on children's schooling.

The family may look different today, but parents continue to care about their children. Teachers care about the achievement of their students. Both have more abilities and potential to do a more successful job than ever before. These are strengths that policymakers can build upon.

APPENDIX F. EDUCATIONAL PARTNERSHIPS

EDUCATION REQUIRES PARTNERSHIPS AMONG STAFF, STUDENTS, AND COMMUNITY*

by William J. Simpson and Sandra Simpson

Timing may be important, but in education attitude is everything.

Consider why some schools succeed while others fail. Attitude toward teaching and learning often separates the successful school from the nonsuccessful school.

Attitude, put simply, is approach—approach to teaching, approach to learning, approach to interacting with one another, etc. What we do becomes almost secondary to *how* we do it.

We can take steps to bring about change, but the onus of responsibility must be shared equally by *all* involved. Positive attitude *must* be contagious. When teachers, administrators, students, parents, community members, and business representatives become committed allies, educational battlefields can be turned into halls of learning once again.

BUILDING PARTNERSHIPS

Active participation and shared responsibility demonstrate a true commitment to education. Achievement occurs only when the participants feel they have a vested interest in the school and the educational process occurring within it. Regardless of how much money is spent on new programs or other innovations, no gains will be made until this vested interest is developed.

As a support system, the community-at-large provides a wealth of resources upon which the school can draw. Each time we use

---

*From *NJEA Review*, May 1987. Copyright © 1987 by the New Jersey Education Associaton. Reprinted with permission.

these resources and positive results occur, additional resources become available. Consequently the school and community are drawn closer together.

The positive ramifications of working together are unlimited. Administrators who are willing to take the "risk" of involving the community and who solicit assistance from these previously untapped sources will find new avenues of support opening up. Businesses and public organizations can become extensions of the classroom, providing students with unique learning experiences. In addition, businesses may be willing to provide some funds for educational materials, equipment, and special projects.

Parental/community visibility in the day-to-day functioning of the school also can provide many positive effects, the most important being the development of an empathetic understanding between school staff and parents.

By becoming part of the school community, parents will appreciate school staff more. Consequently, school employees will feel increased self-esteem, and the importance of what they do in the classroom or elsewhere in the school will be reaffirmed.

Parents, especialy those of inner-city students, can begin to realize that their contributions have a significant impact on the learning process, regardless of their personal levels of educational attainment. Daily parental involvement—through a variety of projects—can reduce disciplinary problems and poor attendance, as well as motivate students to want to do better academically.

Educational partnerships give the private sector the opportunity to demonstrate concern for the community's well-being and boost its public image. Businesses also benefit, gaining a work force that is better educated and prepared to meet its needs, now and in the future.

Good schools help keep communities healthy. Businesses flourish in healthy communities, and healthy communities attract new businesses.

The participants with the most to gain are the students. Learning in a caring environment fosters in students the desire to achieve and kindles a school spirit of working toward a common goal. This spirit encourages students to develop a sense of responsibility for their education. Let's face it, regardless of the foundations laid by teachers, administrators, parents, and community members, the ultimate responsibility for learning rests with the students themselves.

Students should not be exempt from meeting their educational responsibilities because of their youth, inexperience, or disadvantaged background. Instead, the school and the community are responsible for providing an atmosphere which facilitates learning and encourages students to nurture a responsible attitude toward learning. Students must come to realize that they are the most important members of the educational team, and they *do* have a vested interest in the school and what takes place within its confines.

THE SCHOLASTIC OLYMPICS

No "quick fixes" exist for bringing about school/community participation. Lasting results require determination and a great deal of hard work. One approach which may bring together the school and community in mutual involvement is using what could be called the "Scholastic Olympics."

Patterned after the famed athletic competition, the Scholastic Olympics pit grades within a school or schools within a district against one another in healthy competition. The Scholastic Olympics are structured so that the students compete on a variety of levels. Students, teachers, administrators, parents, and community members work together as a team, while learning and having fun.

Competition is the catalyst that makes the Scholastic Olympics work, but winning or losing is not the most important feature. The Scholastic Olympics are designed to ensure that everyone wins. The various categories of competition provide a multitude of areas in which each team can succeed.

Categories could include:
- *most improved academic achievement*. Teams are judged on academic *improvement*, by comparing the final grades from the marking period in which the competition takes place with those of another marking period. This way, students whose grades are generally low can easily show improvement, while students who do well can always do better.
- *best attendance*. The team with the highest percentage of students in attendance for a given period of time wins this

category. One marking period may be used.
- *fewest disciplinary infractions.* A record of disciplinary infractions is maintained by the school disciplinarian or administrator in charge of discipline. The team with the fewest number of student infractions in a given period of time wins.
- *community project.* Each team is responsible for developing and implementing a project or projects to benefit the community. Community organizations and local government agencies can assist in identifying the needs of the community. Possible project targets could include senior citizen groups, day care centers, parks and recreation areas, shelters, clinics and hospitals, and the Red Cross. Evaluation in this area could be in terms of hours spent on the project(s) or money raised. With regard to the community project aspect of the competition, even the "losing" teams are winners.
- *athletic competition.* Teams can square off in any sport or sports of their choosing in a mini-"Olympics."
- *music, art, literature, and science competitions.* Teams compete in such areas as vocal, instrumental, dance, drama, poetry, prose, painting, drawing, and sculpting, as well as projects in general science, physics, and biology.

The framework above may be modified to meet the specific needs of the participating school or system.

Community members, business leaders and parents can serve as project consultants, team coordinators, and supporters. They can also provide incentives (awards, prizes, and parties) for the winners and other participants. Once parents and community members see positive results, their continued participation is almost assured.

What we now face, especially in urban school districts, are the hard, cold realities of educational systems which need help. We can help turn the situation around rather than throw up our hands in desperation. True change requires a solid commitment to convert words into actions.

William J. Simpson has been an English teacher at Grace A. Dunn Junior High School in Trenton for 15 years. Sandra Simpson is a former Trenton bilingual teacher.

BIBLIOGRAPHY

1. Benson, P. "New Picture of Families Emerges from Research." *Common Focus* 6, no. 1 (1985). Chapel Hill, N.C.: Center for Early Adolescence.
2. Besharov, D. J., and Dally, M. M. "How Much Are Working Mothers Working?" *Public Opinion* 9, no. 4 (November/December 1986), citing Bureau of Labor Statistics and Census Bureau Reports for March 1986.
3. Bronfenbrenner, Urie. *Is Early Intervention Effective? A Report on Longitudinal Evaluations of Preschool Programs*. Vol. II. Washington, D.C.: Department of Health, Education and Welfare, 1974.
4. Burks, Gladys E. "An Analysis of the Cost Effectiveness of Title I Pull-Out Instruction in the Benton Harbor Area Schools." Benton Harbor, Michigan, Schools, 1978.
5. Burns, J. *The Study of Parental Involvement in Four Federal Education Programs: Executive Summary*. Washington, D.C.: Department of Education, Office of Planning, Budget and Evaluation, 1982.
6. Coleman, James S. and others. *Equality of Educational Opportunity*. Office of Education, Department of Health, Education and Welfare. Washington, D.C.: U.S. Government Printing Office, 1966.
7. Collins, C. H.; Moles, O. C.; and Cross, M. *The Home-School Connection: Selected Partnership Programs in Large Cities*. Boston: Institute for Responsive Education, 1982.
8. Dave, R. J. "The Identification and Measurement of Environment Process Variables That Are Related to Educational Achievement." Doctoral dissertation, University of Chicago, 1963.
9. Education Commission of the States. *Education Advisory, 1985*. Denver, Colo.: the Commission, 1985.
10. *Education Week*. "Report Assesses Elementary Curriculum Trends, Time on Task." March 3, 1985, p. 10.
11. Epstein, J. "Improving American Education: Roles for Parents." Testimony for the Select Committee on Children,

Youth and Families. Washington, D.C.: U.S. House of Representatives, 1984.
12. _____. *Effects on Parents of Teacher Practices in Parent Involvement.* Baltimore: Center for Social Organization of Schools, Johns Hopkins University, 1983.
13. Espinoza, R. "Work and Family Life Among Anglo, Black and Mexican-American Single-Parent Families: Executive Summary." Austin, Tex.: Southwest Educational Development Laboratory, 1983.
14. Goodson, Barbara, and Hess, Robert. *Parents as Teachers of Young Children: An Evaluative Review of Some Contemporary Concepts and Programs.* Palo Alto, Calif: Stanford University, 1975.
15. Gordon, Ira; Olmsted, Patricia; Rubin Robert; and True, Joan. *Continuity Between Home and School: Aspects of Parent Involvement in Follow Through.* Chapel Hill, N.C.: University of North Carolina Press, 1979.
16. Gotts, E. *Summary of Report: Characteristics of Families with Special Needs in Relation to Schools.* Charleston, W. Va.: Appalachia Educational Laboratory, 1982.
17. Hetherington, E. M.; Featherman, D. L.; and Camara, K. A. "Intellectual Functioning and Achievement of Children in One-Parent Households." Paper prepared for National Institute of Education, Washington, D.C., 1981.
18. Heyns, B. "The Influence of Parents' Work on Children's School Achievement." In *Families That Work: Children in a Changing World*, edited by S. B. Kamerman and C. D. Hayes. Washington, D.C.: National Academy Press, 1982.
19. Home and School Institute. *Work, School and Family . . . at the Crossroads.* Washington, D.C.: the Institute, 1984.
20. _____. *Final Report: Parent-School Partnership Project.* Washington, D.C.: Department of Education, 1983.
21. _____. *Families Learning Together Report.* Washington, D.C.: the Institute, 1979.
22. Kagan, Sharon Lynn. *Parent Involvement Research: A Field in Search of Itself.* Boston: Institute for Responsive Education, 1984.
23. Kamerman, S. B., and Hayes, C. D., eds. *Families That Work: Children in a Changing World.* Washington, D.C.:

National Academy Press, 1982.
24. Landsmann, Leanna. "Interview with Arthur Wise." *Instructor Magazine*, March 1985.
25. Linney, J. A., and Vernberg, E. "Changing Patterns of Parental Employment and the Family-School Relationships." In *Children of Working Parents: Experiences and Outcomes*, edited by Cheryl D. Hayes and Sheila B. Kamerman. Washington, D.C.: National Academy Press, 1983.
26. Long, Thomas, and Long, Lynette. *Handbook for Latchkey Children and Their Parents*. New York: Arbor House, 1983.
27. Mason, T., and Espinoza, R. *Final Interim Report: Working Parents Project*. Austin, Tex.: Southwest Educational Development Laboratory, 1983.
28. Medrich, E., and others. *The Serious Business of Growing Up*. Berkeley: University of California Press, 1982.
29. Milne, A., and Ginsburg, A. *Single Parents, Working Mothers and the Educational Achievement of School Children*. Washington, D.C.: Decision Resources, 1985.
30. Naisbitt, John. *Megatrends*. New York: Warner Books, 1983.
31. National Center for Educational Statistics. "Parent and Family Characteristics of 1982 High School Seniors." High School and Beyond Survey. Washington, D.C.: the Center, 1984. Unpublished tabulation.
32. National Education Association. *Estimates of School Statistics, 1985-86*. Washington, D.C.: the Association, 1986.
33. _____. "Report on Teacher-Parent Partnership Project." Washington, D.C.: the Association, 1985.
34. _____. *Nationwide Teacher Opinion Poll, 1983*. Washington, D.C.: the Association, 1983.
35. _____. *Nationwide Teacher Opinion Poll, 1982*. Washington, D.C.: the Association, 1982.
36. _____. *Nationwide Teacher Opinion Poll, 1981*. Washington, D.C.: the Association, 1981.
37. _____. *Nationwide Teacher Opinion Poll, 1980*. Washington, D.C.: the Association, 1980.
38. *New York Times*. "Head Start at 20"; July 4, 1985.
39. Phi Delta Kappa. *Gallup Polls of Attitudes Toward Education, 1969-84*. Bloomington, Ind.: Phi Delta Kappa, 1984.
40. *Phi Delta Kappan*. "1985 Rating of the Public Schools."

September 1985, pp. 36-47.
41. Plaskett, Bernard. *AHEAD Report* (Accelerating Home Education and Development). Los Angeles: Southern Christian Leadership Conference West, 1978.
42. Rich, Dorothy. "The Relationship of the Home Learning Lab Technique to First Grade Student Achievement." Doctoral dissertation, Catholic University of America, 1976.
43. Rich, Spencer. "Poverty Rate Drops Sharply." *Washington Post*, August 28, 1985, p. 1.
44. _____. "One-Parent Families Found to Increase Sharply in U.S." *Washington Post*, May 15, 1985.
45. Schweinhart, L. *Early Childhood Development Programs in the Eighties*. Ypsilanti, Mich.: High-Scope Press, 1985.
46. Stanford Research Institute. *Parent Involvement in Compensatory Education Programs*. Washington, D.C.: Office of Education, Department of Health, Education and Welfare, 1973.
47. Trinity College. *Interim Report: Trinity/Arlington Teacher and Parent Training for School Success Project*. Washington, D.C.: Department of Education, Bilingual Education Office, 1984.
48. Wagenaar, Theodore C. "School Achievement Level vis-à-vis Community Involvement and Support: An Empirical Assessment." Paper presented at annual meeting of American Sociological Association, Ohio State University, Columbus, 1977.
49. Wallerstein, J. S., and Kelly, J. B. *Surviving the Breakup: How Children and Parents Cope with Divorce*. New York: Basic Books, 1980.
50. Williams, D. L. *Parent Involvement in Education: What a Survey Reveals*. Austin, Tex.: Southwest Educational Development Laboratory, 1984.
51. Wilson, J., and Hernstein, R. *Crime and Human Nature*. New York: Simon and Schuster, 1985.
52. Zigler, Edward "Overview of Child Care." Testimony for the Select Committee on Children, Youth and Families. Washington, D.C.: U.S. House of Representatives, 1984.

SELECTED RESOURCES FOR FURTHER STUDY

The following resources are available from the Home and School Institute (Special Projects Office, 1201 16th Street, NW, Washington, DC 20036):

Bright Idea
Problem solving for home concerns: communication, health, money, and household organization. (Pre–K through grade 6)

Families Learning Together
Simultaneous learning for adults and children in reading and arithmetic. (K–6)

Get Smart: Advice for Teens with Babies
Problem-solving manual for teenage mothers: strategies for young mothers as parents and as people with jobs.

Job Success Begins at Home
Skills and attitudes needed for getting and keeping a job. (Grades 4-9)

101 Activities for More Effective School-Community Involvement
Activities for innovative back-to-school nights and parent-teacher events. (Pre–K through grade 8)

Senior Corps Program
Complete, coordinated services of reading, arithmetic, and health learning activities for senior aides working with special needs students and their families. (Grades 5-8)

Special Solutions
Special-help activities for children in arithmetic, reading, writing, science, and social studies. (K–6)

Survival Guide for Busy Parents
Handbook for teaching children at home, combined with tips on managing home and job responsibilities. (K–6)

Three R's Plus
Hundreds of home learning activities concentrating on the basic skills. (Pre–K through grade 8)

ADDITIONAL READINGS

Cattermole J., and Robinson, N. "Effective Home/School Communications—from the Parents' Perspective." *Phi Delta Kappan* 67, no. 1 (September 1985): 48-50.

Comer, James. "Parent Participation in the Schools." *Phi Delta Kappan* 67, no. 6 (February 1986): 442-46.

Commission on Reading. *Becoming a Nation of Readers*. Washington, D.C.: National Academy of Education, National Institute of Education and Center for the Study of Reading, 1985.

Compton, Nancy; Duncan, Mara; and Hruska, Jack. *How Schools Can Help Combat Student Pregnancy*. Washington, D.C.: National Education Association, 1987.

Futrell, Mary Hatwood. "Statement of the National Education Association on Parent Involvement and Choice Before the National Governors' Task Force on Parent Involvement and Choice." Washington, D.C.: National Education Association, December 1986.

Gray, S. T. "How to Create a Successful School/Community Partnership." *Phi Delta Kappan* 65, no. 6 (February 1984): 405-9.

Hodgkinson, Harold, L. *All One System*. Washington, D.C.: Institute for Educational Leadership, 1985.

Instructor Magazine. "Here's What You Care About Most!" May 1986.

Levin, Henry M. *Educational Reform for Disadvantaged Students: An Emerging Crisis*. NEA Search. Washington, D.C.: National Education Association, 1986.

Levine, Michael P. *How Schools Can Help Combat Student Eating Disorders: Anorexia Nervosa and Bulimia*. Washington, D.C.: National Education Association, 1987.

Rich, D. K. *The Forgotten Factor in School Success—The Family*. Washington, D.C.: Home and School Institute, 1985.

Stevenson, Harold; Shin-ying, Lee; and Stingler, James W. "Mathematics Achievement of Chinese, Japanese, and American Children." *Science* (February 14, 1986):693-99.

Tower, Cynthia Crosson. *How Schools Can Help Combat Child Abuse and Neglect*. 2d ed. Washington, D.C.: National Education Association, 1987.

Towers, Richard L. *How Schools Can Help Combat Student Drug and Alcohol Abuse*. Washington, D.C.: National Education Association, 1987.

U.S. Department of Education. *What Works*. Washington, D.C.: U.S. Government Printing Office, 1986.

Walberg, H. J. "Families as Partners in Educational Productivity." *Phi Delta Kappan* 65, no. 6 (February 1984): 397-400.